the
mexican
kitchen

the
mexican
kitchen

ENTICING TASTES FROM A
HOT AND SPICY CUISINE

ELISABETH LAMBERT ORTIZ

LORENZ BOOKS

This edition published by Lorenz Books
27 West 20th Street, New York, NY 10011

LORENZ BOOKS are available for the bulk purchase for sales promotion
and for premium use. For details, write or call the sales director,
Lorenz Books, 27 West 20th Street, New York, NY 10011; (800) 354-9657

Lorenz Books is an imprint of Anness Publishing Inc.

ISBN 1 85967 838 6

Publisher: Joanna Lorenz
Senior Cookery Editor: Linda Fraser
Copy Editor: Jenni Fleetwood
Designer: Siân Keogh
Photography: David Jordan
Food for photography and styling: Judy Williams, assisted by Manisha Kanani
Illustrator: Madeleine David

Front cover: Lisa Tai, Designer; Thomas Odulate, Photographer;
Helen Trent, Stylist; Lucy McKelvie, Home Economist

Previously published as *Taste of Mexico*

Printed in Hong Kong/China

© Anness Publishing Limited 1998, 1999
Updated © 2000
1 3 5 7 9 10 8 6 4 2

CONTENTS

INTRODUCTION

Many of the foods we take for granted in the West were unknown before Christopher Columbus reached the Americas in 1492. The list is impressive. We had never seen corn, tomatoes or peppers (sweet, pungent or hot); or common beans such as red kidneys or pintos, or pumpkins or any other winter squashes. Zucchini and chayotes (chocho) were equally unfamiliar, as were avocados and guavas, and we had never tasted the now ubiquitous chocolate and vanilla. Even turkeys were unknown. All these foods originated in Mexico, where agriculture is believed to have been practiced as long ago as 7000 BC, about the same time, give or take a century or two, as the cultivation of food crops began in the Middle East.

After the Conquest of Mexico by Hernán Cortés, the Spanish introduced wheat and domesticated animals, hitherto unknown in the Americas. Cattle yielded beef, milk, butter, cream and cheese. The domestic pig, being better to eat, soon ousted the local wild and wily boar and lambs; goats and the domestic hen made their appearance. The Spanish planted olive trees for olive oil, and walnut trees, as well as the vegetables that reminded them of home. It was out of this meeting of Old and New Worlds that the cuisine of Mexico developed. This colonial kitchen still rests firmly on its Aztec and Mayan foundations, and though it is unique in the world of cooking, it is neither difficult nor inaccessible.

There are no difficult or complicated techniques to master, and the unique flavors of Mexican dishes appeal to nearly everyone.

When the Spanish priest Father Bernadinho Sahagun visited Mexico at the beginning of the conquest (from 1519–21), he was deeply impressed by the great central market in the Aztec capital. He wrote about the foods he found there, describing the various types of unleavened flat pancakes made from corn flour, which the Spanish called *tortillas*. This bread has the distinction of being made from cooked flour. Dried corn kernels are cooked in water with lime until soft, when the skins can be rubbed off. The corn is drained and ground to a heavy paste. It is sold at the markets to make tortillas, or dried and packaged as *masa harina*, literally "dough flour." Tortillas are easy enough to make at home using a tortilla press, which consists of two hinged circles of wood or metal. A ball of dough is placed on the bottom circle, then the top is brought down, flattening it to a round, which is then baked for a minute or two on a *comal*

The varied terrains of Mexico give a diverse harvest: seafood from the coast, beef from the north and corn from the central plateau.

GULF OF MEXICO

Monterrey

Guadalajara

Mexico City   Veracruz

PACIFIC OCEAN

Acapulco

or a griddle. Although many Mexican women still make tortillas at home, some using the ancient skill of patting them out by hand, they can also be purchased uncooked or freshly baked from *tortillerias*. Tortillas are also exported; you can now buy them in most supermarkets. They are used as the basis of a number of dishes that the Spanish call *antojitos*. More than just snack foods or appetizers, these little whims or fancies form a whole category in the Mexican kitchen.

Of equal importance in Mexican cooking is the family of cultivated capsicums that the Aztecs collectively called chili although we tend to differentiate between chilies and the mild-flavored red, yellow and green bell peppers. It is estimated there may be over a hundred varieties of chilies, some sold fresh, others pickled or dried. Chilies can irritate delicate skin: it is vital to wash your hands in warm, soapy water immediately after handling them. Cooks with particularly sensitive skin should wear rubber gloves.

The tomato is another ingredient essential to Mexican cooking, whether raw or cooked. There is another Mexican tomato, the green-husked tomatillo (*Physalis ixocarpa*), which has an exquisite flavor. It is widely used in Mexico but has never been as popular elsewhere as the red, true tomato, except in Guatemala.

The Mexican kitchen is strongly regional. The cattle country of the north, bordering on Texas, is not good corn country, and here the wheat flour tortilla is popular. It is always eaten with roast kid (baby goat), a northern favorite, and *salsa verde* made with the tomatillo.

Much of the country is at altitudes of 7,000 to 8,000 feet. Here the climate is temperate and all manner of fruits and vegetables flourish on the high plateau. The town of Puebla is famous for exquisite crystallized fruit, including small, juicy and delicious peaches. Puebla is also the home of that

The unique blend of Old and New World customs, produce and lifestyles is evident in this colorful Oaxaca street scene.

great festival dish, *Mole Poblano de Guajolote*. The flavors in the sauce blend well in the long cooking time dictated by the high altitude.

The semi-tropical regions at sea level have abundant tropical fruits and vegetables, including pawpaws (papayas), pineapples and coconuts. The extensive coastline yields a rich harvest of fish and shellfish. Before the Aztecs dominated the country, the Mayan Empire had flourished, invading Mexico's Yucatán peninsula and the southern part of the country. Here the cooking is subtly different. There are many regional chilies as well as unique herbs and spices. *Achiote* (annatto) is especially popular. The area boasts a sauce, *Ixni-pec* (pronounced Schnee-peck), made with the *habanero* chili – the hottest chili in North America.

The ancient art of cooking in an earth oven still flourishes in Mexico. For *barbacoa* in the plateau, a pit is lined with the leaves of the agave plant. Heated stones are placed in the pit, the food (a whole lamb, vegetables and so on) is arranged on top, the pit is then sealed and the food is left to cook. The

agave gives a subtle flavor of tequila to the foods. In the Yucatán the earth oven is called a *pib*. It is lined with banana leaves, and the meat, a suckling pig, or maybe a chicken, is seasoned with *achiote* among other flavorings, and sprinkled with Seville orange juice, before being sealed in the pit and cooked.

In spite of industrialization, most people in Mexico prefer to eat their main meal, *comida*, in the middle of the day. This is a long, late lunch, often followed by a siesta. Soup is a must and so are beans. A small dish of beans (usually red kidney or pinto) are served separately after the main course and before dessert, which is often just fresh fruit. Breakfast is coffee with milk and a sweet bread. *Almuerzo*, a light meal which often bridges the gap between breakfast and *comida,* usually consists of a corn-based dish, and although there may be a proper dinner, *cena*, served very late, more often the last meal is a light supper, *merienda*. This is often comprised of tamales and atole (corn gruel), possibly with the addition of some sweet breads and jam.

INGREDIENTS

ACHIOTE (ANNATTO)
Prized for its flavoring and coloring qualities, this comes from the hard orange-red coating around the seeds of the small tropical American flowering tree *Bixa orellana*. The pulp, dissolved in oil or water, imparts a delicate flavor and a deep, golden-orange color. The small seeds are ground for use as a flavoring.

AVOCADOS
The avocado, which is now grown all over the world, originated in Central America. It was named after the Aztec *ahuacatl,* which the Spanish called *aguacate*. The Mexican avocado has a thin skin, small fruit, anise-scented leaves, a high oil content, and is the hardest. The Haas avocado, grown in California, is a good stand-in.

BEANS
Dried beans (*frijoles*) are a staple in the Mexican diet, either served with a little of the cooking liquid, or mashed and fried with lard or oil as refritos. Pink, red and black beans are native to Mexico, as are speckled pinto beans. Also popular are lima beans from Peru, and garbanzos (also known as chick-peas) which come from the Middle East. In addition there are *ejotes* which are fresh green beans.

Clockwise from top left: dried chick-peas, dried kidney beans, fresh green beans and dried pinto beans.

Clockwise from top left: small green chilies, chipotle chilies, *mulato* chilies, *dried habanero* chilies, *pasilla* chilies, *green peppers, green* jalapeño *peppers,* anaheim chilies, *and (center left) fresh* habanero chilies, *(center right) fresh red chilies.*

CHAYOTE (CHRISTOPHINE OR CHOCHO)
A small squash indigenous to Mexico, the chayote is round or pear-shaped, light green in color and may be smooth or corrugated. Delicately flavored, it has a firm, crisp flesh and large edible seed. Chayotes are widely used as a vegetable accompaniment or in soups or salads.

CHILIES AND PEPPERS
These are indigenous to Mexico and there are innumerable varieties. The most commonly used fresh green chilies are *serrano, jalapeño* and *poblano,* all hot. The *habanero* (Scotch Bonnet) is small, flavorful and the hottest chili in North America. It may be red or green and is used fresh. The most popular dried chilies are *ancho* (full-flavored and mild) and *chipotle* (very hot). Other varieties include the *mulato,* which is pungent and the hot *pasilla*. In addition there are the large, bell-shaped sweet bell peppers (hence the name). These may be green, yellow or red, depending on their ripeness, and they are not hot. Canned or bottled red peppers are called pimientos.

CHOCOLATE
Chocolate originated in Mexico thousands of years ago. It was drunk as a hot or cold, foam-topped flavored drink. Today Mexican chocolate is sold in blocks flavored with cinnamon, almonds and vanilla and is used in drinks and cooking.

CHORIZO
A highly seasoned, reddish-colored link sausage which is used a great deal in Mexican cooking. It comes in many varieties, but all have pork and paprika in common which gives them their distinctive color. Some varieties are hotter than others.

CILANTRO (FRESH CORIANDER)
This green feathery herb resembles Italian flat-leaf parsley or chervil in appearance and is widely used in Mexican cooking. It is an essential ingredient of guacamole. The seeds are less widely used.

CORN
Corn was one of the first plants cultivated in Mexico and is extremely important. The dried kernels are ground to make *masa harina* (dough flour), which is used to make tortillas, tamales and a host of other small baked goods, and the drink atole.

Clockwise from top left: mint, cilantro, flat-leaf parsley, oregano and bay leaves.

Clockwise from top left: avocados, string of garlic, chayotes, garlic bulb, tomatoes, onions, tomatillos and canned jalapeño *peppers (in a bowl), zucchini, lemons and lime halves (center).*

known as "husk tomatoes" because of their papery covering. They are often sold fresh and are available canned in the Mexican section of most supermarkets. Tomatillos have an exquisite and distinctive flavor and are used in sauces and in the "green" dishes. They must be cooked for a few minutes for their full flavor to develop.

CORN DISHES (ANTOJITOS)

Corn plays a very important role in the Mexican kitchen and is central to the dishes the Spanish dubbed *antojitos* (little whims or fancies), which are eaten as snacks or light lunches. Some, like tacos, are very simple; others, such as enchiladas, are more elaborate. Tamales consist of steamed dried corn husks or banana leaves with a dough and meat filling. All these dishes are based on *masa harina*, flour made from dried corn boiled in lime water before being ground.

GUACAMOLE

There are many recipes for this classic salsa. In its simplest form it is made by mashing avocados with a squeeze or two of lime or lemon juice, a handful of chopped cilantro, a little crushed garlic, chopped scallions, salt, and chopped fresh *serrano* chilies.

Clockwise from top left: pumpkin seeds, star anise, masa harina, *flour, cinnamon sticks, Mexican chocolate and almonds.*

FLOR DE JAMAICA (ROSELLA OR SORREL)

This is a tropical plant grown for its fleshy red sepals, which are used to make a soft drink in Mexico called Aqua de Jamaica (Jamaica Water).

NOPALES/NOPALITOS (PRICKLY PEAR CACTUS PADDLES)

These are the paddles of the prickly pear cactus. The prickly pear can be either red or yellow in color and is covered in thorns. The cactus paddles are removed and cleaned before being diced and either canned or bottled. In the Mexican kitchen they are used as a vegetable, in salads, soups and omelets. The plant bears delicious fruit called "tunas" which are sold fresh in Mexican markets.

PILONCILLO (MEXICAN SUGAR)

This unrefined dark brown cane sugar is sold in cone-shaped loaves. It tastes like molasses and is used to sweeten desserts and coffee. Dark brown sugar is a good substitute.

PEPITAS (DRIED PUMPKIN SEEDS)

These are small, plump, delicately-flavored seeds. Buy the hulled pumpkin seeds that are available in health food stores and delicatessens. Ground to a powder, the seeds are used to flavor and thicken sauces.

TOMATILLOS (MEXICAN GREEN TOMATOES)

These are not unripe ordinary tomatoes but come from a different plant, *Physalis ixocarpa*. They are sometimes

CORN DISHES

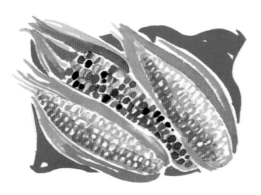

Corn plays a very important role in the Mexican kitchen and is central to the dishes the Spanish dubbed antojitos *(little whims or fancies), which are eaten as snacks or light lunches. Some, like tacos, are very simple; others, such as enchiladas, are more elaborate. Tamales consist of steamed dried corn husks or banana leaves with a dough and meat filling. All these dishes are based on* masa harina, *flour made from dried corn boiled in lime water before being ground.*

Corn Tortillas

Before you start making tortillas, be sure to have a tortilla press ready. Cut open a small plastic sandwich bag along its side and bottom seams.

INGREDIENTS

Makes about fourteen 5½-inch tortillas
2 cups *masa harina* (tortilla flour)
1–1½ cups water

COOK'S TIP

Tortillas are very easy to make, but it is important to get the dough texture right. If it is too dry and crumbly, add a little water; if it is too wet, add more *masa harina*. If you misjudge the pressure needed for flattening the ball of dough to a neat circle on the tortilla press, just scrape it off, re-roll it and try again.

1 Put the *masa harina* into a bowl and stir in 1 cup of the water, mixing to a soft dough that just holds together. If it is too dry, add a little more water. Cover the bowl with a cloth and set aside for 15 minutes.

2 Preheat the oven to 300°F. Open the tortilla press and line both sides with the prepared plastic sheets. Preheat a griddle until hot.

3 Knead the dough lightly and shape into 14 balls. Put a ball on the press and bring the top down firmly to flatten the dough out into a round.

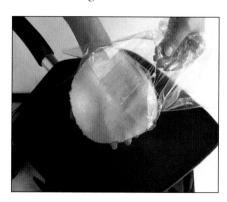

4 Open the press. Peel off the top layer of plastic and lift the tortilla by means of the bottom plastic. Turn it onto your palm, so that the plastic is on top. Peel off the plastic and flip the tortilla onto the hot griddle.

5 Cook for about 1 minute or until the edges start to curl. Turn over and cook for another minute. Wrap in foil and keep warm in the oven.

Flour Tortillas

INGREDIENTS

Makes about fourteen 6-inch tortillas
2 cups all-purpose flour
1 teaspoon salt
1 tablespoon lard or vegetable
shortening

1 Sift the flour and salt into a mixing bowl. Rub in the lard with your fingertips until the mixture resembles coarse breadcrumbs.

2 Gradually add ½ cup water and mix to a soft dough. Knead lightly, form into a ball, cover the bowl with a cloth and let rest for 15 minutes.

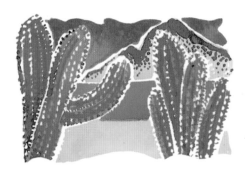

3 Divide the dough into about 14 portions and form into balls. Roll out each ball of dough on a lightly floured board to a round measuring about 6 inches. Trim the rounds if necessary.

COOK'S TIP

Make flour tortillas whenever *masa harina* is hard to find. To keep them soft and pliable, make sure they are kept warm.

4 Heat a medium-size, ungreased griddle or heavy frying pan over medium heat. Cook the tortillas, one at a time, for 1½–2 minutes on each side. Turn over with a large metal spatula when the bottom becomes a delicate brown. Adjust the heat if the tortilla browns too quickly.

5 Stack the tortillas in a clean cloth if eating right away. Otherwise wrap in foil and keep warm in the oven.

Mixed Tostadas

Like little edible plates, these golden crisp-fried tortillas can support any toppings that are not too juicy.

INGREDIENTS

Makes 14
oil, for shallow frying
14 freshly prepared unbaked
    corn tortillas
1 cup mashed red kidney or pinto
    beans
1 head iceberg lettuce, shredded
oil and vinegar dressing (optional)
2 cooked chicken breasts, skinned and
    thinly sliced
1 cup Guacamole (see Index)
1 cup coarsely grated Cheddar cheese
pickled *jalapeño* peppers, seeded and
    sliced, to taste

1 Heat the oil in a frying pan and fry the tortillas until golden brown on both sides and crisp but not hard.

2 Spread each tortilla with a layer of beans. Put a layer of shredded lettuce (which can be left plain or lightly tossed with a little dressing) over the beans.

3 Arrange pieces of chicken in a layer on top of the lettuce. Carefully spread over a layer of the guacamole and finally sprinkle over a layer of the grated cheese.

4 Arrange the mixed tostadas on a large platter. Serve on individual plates, but eat using your hands.

Quesadillas

These delicious filled and deep-fried tortilla turnovers make a popular snack, and smaller versions make excellent canapés.

INGREDIENTS

Makes 14
14 freshly prepared tortillas

For the filling
1 cup finely chopped or grated
    Cheddar cheese
3 *jalapeño* peppers, seeded and cut
    into strips
oil, for frying
salt

1 Have the tortillas ready, covered with a clean cloth. Combine the grated cheese and chili strips in a bowl. Season with salt. Set aside.

2 Heat the oil in a frying pan. Then, holding an unbaked tortilla on your palm, put a spoonful of filling along the center, avoiding the edges.

> ——— COOK'S TIP ———
>
> For other stuffings, try leftover beans with chilies or chopped chorizo sausage fried with a little chopped onion.

3 Fold the tortilla and seal the edges by pressing or crimping together. Fry in hot oil, on both sides, until golden brown and crisp.

4 Using a spatula, lift out the quesadilla and drain it on paper towels. Transfer to a plate and keep warm while frying the remaining quesadillas. Serve hot.

Tortilla Flutes

Flutes, or *flautas,* look as good as they taste.

Ingredients

Makes about 12

24 freshly prepared unbaked
  flour tortillas
2 tomatoes, peeled, seeded
  and chopped
1 small onion, chopped
1 garlic clove, chopped
2–3 tablespoons corn oil
2 freshly cooked chicken breasts,
  skinned and shredded
salt

To garnish
sliced radishes
stuffed green olives

1 Place the unbaked flour tortillas in pairs on a work surface, with the right-hand tortilla overlapping its partner by about 2 inches.

2 Put the tomatoes, onion, and garlic into a food processor and process to a purée. Season with salt to taste.

3 Heat 1 tablespoon of the oil in a frying pan and cook the tomato purée for a few minutes, stirring to blend the flavors. Remove from the heat and stir in the shredded chicken, mixing well.

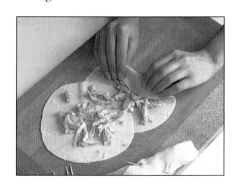

4 Spread about 2 tablespoons of the chicken mixture on each pair of tortillas, roll them up into flutes and secure with a toothpick.

5 Heat a little oil in a frying pan large enough to hold the flutes comfortably. Cook more than one at a time if possible, but don't overcrowd the pan. Fry the flutes until light brown all over. Add more oil if needed.

6 Drain the cooked flutes on paper towels and keep hot. When ready to serve, transfer to a platter and garnish with radishes and olives.

COOK'S TIP

If the flour tortillas are too hard to roll up easily, fry them for just a few seconds in hot oil, then quickly stuff and roll them.

Chilaquiles

INGREDIENTS

Serves 4

corn or peanut oil, for frying
6 leftover corn tortillas, cut or torn into
   ¹/₂-inch strips
10-ounce can tomatillos (Mexican
   green tomatoes)
1 onion, finely chopped
2–3 drained canned *jalapeño* peppers,
   rinsed, seeded and chopped
2 tablespoons chopped fresh cilantro
1 cup grated Cheddar cheese
³/₄ cup chicken stock
salt and freshly ground black pepper

To garnish

chopped scallion
stuffed green olives
chopped cilantro

1 Heat 3 tablespoons of the oil in a large frying pan. Fry the tortilla strips, a few at a time, on both sides, without browning. Add more oil if needed. Drain on paper towels.

2 Place the tomatillos and juice in a food processor. Add the onion, *jalapeños* and cilantro; purée.

3 Season the tomatillo purée with salt and pepper. Heat 1 tablespoon oil in the clean frying pan, add the tomatillo mixture and cook gently for 2–3 minutes, stirring frequently.

4 Pour a layer of the sauce into the bottom of a flameproof casserole or shallow baking dish and top with a layer of tortilla strips and a layer of grated cheese. Continue until all the ingredients have been used, reserving some cheese for sprinkling on top.

5 Pour the chicken stock over the dish and sprinkle with the reserved cheese. If using a flameproof casserole, cover and cook over medium heat until all the liquid has been absorbed and the chilaquiles are heated through. Or bake the chilaquiles, uncovered, in a preheated 350°F oven for 30 minutes, or until heated through.

6 Serve directly from the casserole, garnished with chopped scallions, olives and cilantro.

Tamales de Picadillo

In ancient times, these little packages of corn were cooked in the hot ashes of a camp fire.

INGREDIENTS

Makes 12
12 dried corn husks
¼ cup lard or vegetable shortening
1 cup *masa harina* (tortilla flour)
½ teaspoon salt
1 teaspoon baking powder
¾ cup chicken stock
½ quantity Picadillo

1 Soak the corn husks in warm water for about 2 hours until pliable.

2 In a bowl, cream the lard until it is very light and fluffy. Mix the *masa harina* with the salt and baking powder and beat it into the lard, bit by bit.

3 Warm the chicken stock. It should not be hot or it will melt the lard. Gradually beat enough stock into the flour mixture to make a mushy dough. To see if the dough is ready, carefully place a small piece on top of a bowl of water. If it floats, the dough is ready; if it sinks, continue to beat the dough until it floats.

4 Drain a corn husk; lay it flat on a board. Spread 2 tablespoons of the dough down the center part of the husk, leaving plenty of room all around for folding. Spoon 2 tablespoons of the Picadillo onto the center of the dough. Roll up the husk from one long side, jelly-roll fashion, so that the filling is completely enclosed, then fold the ends of the husks under. Make more tamales in the same way.

5 Prepare a steamer or use a metal colander and a deep saucepan into which the colander will fit with about 1 inch of space all around.

6 Put the tamales in the steamer, folded ends under. Alternatively, place them in the colander and pour boiling water into the pan to within 1 inch of the bottom of the colander. Steam the tamales for about 1 hour, or until the dough comes away from the husk. Add water as required. Serve the tamales in the husk, letting the diners open them at the table to reveal the filling inside.

VARIATIONS

Any shredded cooked meat, moistened with salsa, can be used in the filling of these *tamales*. Alternatively, use strips of seeded *jalapeño* pepper and Cheddar cheese. If you have any leftover Mole Poblano de Guajolote, use 1½ tablespoons to fill each tamale. *Tamales de Oaxaca* uses banana leaves softened in hot water and cut into 10-inch squares, instead of corn husks.

Red Enchiladas

INGREDIENTS

Serves 6

4 dried *ancho* chilies
1 pound tomatoes, peeled, seeded
   and chopped
1 onion, finely chopped
1 garlic clove, chopped
1 tablespoon chopped fresh cilantro
lard or corn oil for frying
1 cup sour cream
4 chorizo sausages, skinned
   and chopped
18 freshly prepared unbaked
   corn tortillas
2½ cups freshly grated Parmesan
   cheese
salt and freshly ground black pepper

1 Roast the *ancho* chilies in a dry frying pan over moderate heat for 1–2 minutes, shaking the pan frequently. When cool, carefully slit the chilies, remove the stems and seeds, and tear the pods into pieces. Put in a bowl, add warm water to cover, and soak for 20 minutes.

2 Pour the chilies, with a little of the soaking water, into a food processor. Add the tomatoes, onion, garlic and cilantro; purée.

COOK'S TIP

The method of dipping the tortillas first in sauce, then quickly cooking them in lard or oil gives the best flavor. If you prefer, fry the plain tortillas very quickly, then dip them in the sauce, stuff and roll. There is not a great loss of flavor, and no spatter.

3 Heat 1 tablespoon of the lard or oil in a heavy saucepan. Add the purée and cook gently over medium heat, stirring, for 3–4 minutes. Season to taste with salt and pepper and then stir in the sour cream. Remove the pan from the heat and set it aside.

4 Heat another tablespoon of the lard or oil in a small frying pan; sauté the chorizo for a few minutes, until lightly browned. Moisten with a little of the sauce and set the pan aside.

5 Preheat the oven to 350°F. Heat 2 tablespoons of the lard or oil in a frying pan. Dip a tortilla in the sauce and add to the pan. Cook for a few seconds, shaking the pan gently, then turn over and briefly fry the other side.

6 Slide the tortilla onto a plate, top with some of the sausage mixture, and roll up. Pack the prepared tortillas in a single layer in a baking dish. Pour the sauce over, sprinkle with Parmesan and bake for about 20 minutes.

Chimichangas

INGREDIENTS

Makes 14
½ quantity Picadillo
14 freshly prepared unbaked
    flour tortillas
oil, for frying
whole radishes with leaves, to garnish

— COOK'S TIP —

Chimichangas originally came from the state of Sonora and are made with the large plate-sized tortillas that are a speciality of the region. Any size that suits the cook will do just as well.

1 Spoon 4 tablespoons of Picadillo down the center of each tortilla. Fold in the sides, then the top and bottom, envelope-fashion, or simply roll up and secure with a toothpick.

2 Pour the corn oil into a frying pan to a depth of about 1 inch. Set the pan over medium heat. Fry the chimichangas, a few at a time, for 1–2 minutes, or until golden.

3 Drain on paper towels and keep warm. Serve the chimichangas garnished with whole radishes.

Tacos

The taco, a Mexican sandwich, makes a great quick snack. All you need is a supply of tortillas or taco shells, and a selection of fillings. See the Index for recipes.

INGREDIENTS

Makes as many as you like
freshly prepared corn tortillas or
    prepared taco shells

For the fillings

Picadillo topped with Guacamole
chopped chorizo fried and mixed with
    chopped Cheddar cheese and chilies
Frijoles Refritos with sliced *jalapeño*
    peppers, Guacamole, and cubed
    cheese
leftover Mole Poblano de Guajolote
    with Guacamole
cooked shredded pork or chicken with
    salsa and shredded lettuce

1 To make tacos, all you need is a supply of fresh corn tortillas, and as many of the suggested fillings as you can muster. The idea is to use your imagination, and cooks often vie with one another to see who can produce the most interesting combination of flavors. Chilies and guacamole are always welcome, in the taco or served as an extra on the side.

2 To make traditional soft tacos, simply spoon the filling onto the tortilla, wrap the tortilla around the filling – and eat.

3 To make hard tacos, secure the rolled up and filled tortilla with a toothpick, then briefly fry until crisp and golden.

4 Prepared U-shaped taco shells are not Mexican, but make a very fast version of this snack. Hold one taco shell at a time in one hand, and fill with the fillings of your choice.

SOUPS

Soups are a must for the midday main meal, comida. There are two types, aguada (liquid) and seca (dry). The first term is self-explanatory, but what exactly is a dry soup? It describes a separate course – traditionally a tortilla or rice dish – served after the more conventional soup and before the main course. Mexican cooks set great store by the quality of their homemade chicken and beef stocks. Either of these can be served as a soup in its own right with the addition of rice or chick-peas.

Vermicelli Soup

INGREDIENTS

Serves 4

2 tablespoons olive or corn oil
⅓ cup vermicelli
1 onion, coarsely chopped
1 garlic clove, chopped
1 pound tomatoes, peeled, seeded and
   coarsely chopped
4 cups chicken stock
¼ teaspoon sugar
1 tablespoon finely chopped
   fresh cilantro
salt and freshly ground black pepper
chopped fresh cilantro, to garnish
¼ cup freshly grated Parmesan cheese,
   to serve

--- COOK'S TIP ---

Vermicelli burns very easily, so move it
around constantly in the frying pan with a
wooden spoon, and remove it from the heat
as soon as it is golden brown.

1 Heat the oil in a frying pan and
sauté the vermicelli over medium
heat until golden brown. Take care not
to let the strands burn. Remove the
vermicelli with a slotted spoon and
drain on paper towels.

2 Purée the onion, garlic and
tomatoes in a food processor until
smooth. Return the frying pan to the
heat. When the oil is hot, add the
purée. Cook, stirring constantly, for
about 5 minutes, or until thick.

3 Transfer the purée to a saucepan.
Add the vermicelli and pour in
the stock. Season with sugar, salt and
pepper. Stir in the cilantro, bring to a
boil, then lower the heat, cover the
pan and simmer the soup until the
vermicelli is tender.

4 Serve in heated bowls, sprinkle
with chopped fresh cilantro and
pass the Parmesan separately.

Tomato Soup

INGREDIENTS

Serves 4

1 tablespoon corn or peanut oil
1 onion, finely chopped
2 pounds tomatoes, peeled, seeded
   and chopped
2 cups chicken stock
2 large fresh cilantro sprigs
salt and freshly ground black pepper
coarsely ground black pepper, to serve

1 Heat the oil in a large saucepan
and gently fry the finely chopped
onion, stirring frequently, for about
5 minutes, or until it is soft and
transparent but not brown.

2 Add the chopped tomatoes,
chicken stock and cilantro sprigs to
the pan. Bring to a boil, then lower the
heat, cover the pan and simmer gently
for about 15 minutes.

3 Remove and discard the cilantro.
Press the soup through a sieve and
return it to the clean pan. Season and
heat through. Serve sprinkled with
coarsely ground black pepper.

Corn Soup

This is a simple-to-make yet very tasty soup. It is sometimes made with sour cream and cream cheese. *Poblano* chilies may be added, but these are rather difficult to find outside Mexico.

INGREDIENTS

Serves 4
2 tablespoons corn oil
1 onion, finely chopped
1 red pepper, seeded and chopped
1 pound canned or frozen corn,
    thawed if frozen
3 cups chicken stock
½ cup light cream
salt and freshly ground black pepper
½ red bell pepper, seeded and cut in
    small dice, to garnish

1 Heat the oil in a frying pan and sauté the onion and red pepper for about 5 minutes, until soft. Add the corn and sauté for 2 minutes.

2 Carefully pour the contents of the pan into a food processor or blender. Process until smooth, scraping down the sides and adding a little of the stock, if necessary.

3 Put the mixture into a saucepan and stir in the stock. Season to taste with salt and pepper, bring to a simmer and cook for 5 minutes.

4 Gently stir in the cream. Serve the soup hot or chilled, sprinkled with the diced red pepper. If serving hot, reheat gently after adding the cream, but do not allow the soup to boil.

Zucchini Soup

INGREDIENTS

Serves 4
2 tablespoons butter
1 onion, finely chopped
1 pound young zucchini, trimmed and
    chopped
3 cups chicken stock
½ cup light cream, plus extra
    to serve
salt and freshly ground black pepper

--- COOK'S TIP ---

Always use the smallest zucchini available. This is how they are preferred in Mexico, their country of origin.

1 Melt the butter in a saucepan and sauté the onion until it is soft. Add the zucchini and cook, stirring, for about 1–2 minutes.

2 Add the chicken stock. Bring to a boil over medium heat and simmer for about 5 minutes, or until the zucchini are just tender.

3 Strain the stock into a clean saucepan, saving the vegetable solids in the strainer. Purée the solids in a food processor and add to the pan. Season to taste with salt and pepper.

4 Stir the cream into the soup and heat through very gently, without allowing it to boil. Serve hot with a little extra cream swirled in.

Sopa Seca de Tortilla con Crema

Dry soup is a separate course that follows liquid soup (*sopa aguada*) in the main meal or *comida*.

INGREDIENTS

Serves 6

½ cup corn oil
1 onion, finely chopped
2 garlic cloves, chopped
1 pound tomatoes, peeled, seeded and finely chopped
½ teaspoon dried oregano
¼ teaspoon sugar
16 small, day-old corn tortillas, cut into ½-inch strips
1 cup heavy cream
1 cup freshly grated Parmesan cheese
salt and freshly ground black pepper

1 Heat 2 tablespoons of oil in a frying pan. Sauté the onion and garlic until soft and stir in the tomatoes.

— COOK'S TIP —

Be sure to use corn tortillas for this recipe. If only large ones are available, use eight.

2 Cook the tomatoes until thick, then stir in the oregano and sugar. Season and put in a bowl. Set aside.

3 Heat the remaining oil in the clean pan and fry the tortillas without browning. Drain on paper towels.

4 Pour a layer of tomato sauce into a greased flameproof casserole. Add a layer of tortilla strips, a thin layer of cream, another layer of sauce, and a layer of grated cheese. Continue until all the ingredients have been used, ending with a layer of cheese. Cover the casserole and heat through gently on top of the stove. (Or, heat through in a preheated 350°F oven for about 20 minutes.)

Mexican-style Rice

INGREDIENTS

Serves 6

1³/₄ cups long-grain white rice
1 onion, chopped
2 garlic cloves, chopped
1 pound tomatoes, peeled, seeded and
   coarsely chopped
4 tablespoons corn or peanut oil
3³/₄ cups chicken stock
4–6 small red chilies, such
   as *habaneros*
1 cup cooked green peas
salt and freshly ground black pepper
fresh cilantro sprigs, to garnish

1 Soak the rice in a bowl of hot water for 15 minutes. Drain, rinse well under cold running water, drain again and set aside.

2 Combine the onion, garlic and tomatoes in a food processor and process to a purée.

3 Heat the oil in a large frying pan. Add the drained rice and sauté until it is golden brown. Using a slotted spoon, transfer the rice to a saucepan.

4 Reheat the oil remaining in the pan and cook the tomato purée for 2–3 minutes. Add it to the saucepan and pour in the stock. Season to taste. Bring to a boil, reduce the heat to the lowest possible setting, cover the pan, and cook for 15–20 minutes, until almost all the liquid has been absorbed. Slice the red chilies from tip to stem end into four or five sections. Place in a bowl of iced water until they curl back to form flowers, then drain.

5 Stir the peas into the rice mixture and cook, without a lid, until all the liquid has been absorbed and the rice is tender. Stir the mixture from time to time.

6 Transfer the rice to a serving dish and garnish with the drained chili flowers and sprigs of cilantro. Warn diners that these elaborate chili "flowers" are blistering hot and should be approached with caution.

Tlalpeño-style Soup

For a hearty version of this simple soup, add some cooked chick-peas or rice.

INGREDIENTS

Serves 6
6 cups chicken stock
2 cooked chicken breasts, boned, skinned and cut into large strips
1 drained canned *chipotle* or *jalapeño* pepper, rinsed
1 avocado

─── COOK'S TIP ───

When using canned chilies, it is important to rinse them very thoroughly before adding them to the pan, to remove the flavor of any pickling liquid.

1 Heat the stock in a large saucepan and add the chicken and chili. Simmer over very low heat for 5 minutes to heat the chicken and release the flavor from the chili.

2 Cut the avocado in half, remove the pit and peel off the skin. Slice the avocado flesh neatly.

3 Remove the chili from the stock, using a slotted spoon, and then discard it. Pour the soup into heated serving bowls, distributing the chicken evenly among them.

4 Carefully add a few avocado slices to each bowl and serve.

Avocado Soup

INGREDIENTS

Serves 4
2 large ripe avocados
4 cups chicken stock
1 cup light cream
salt and freshly ground white pepper
1 tablespoon finely chopped cilantro, to garnish (optional)

─── COOK'S TIP ───

The easiest way to mash the avocados is to hold each seeded half in the palm of one hand and mash the flesh in the shell with a fork, before scooping it into the bowl. This keeps the avocado from slipping around when it is being mashed.

1 Cut the avocados in half, remove the pits and mash the flesh (see Cook's Tip). Put the flesh into a sieve and, using a wooden spoon, press it through into a warm soup bowl.

2 Heat the chicken stock with the cream in a saucepan. When the mixture is hot, but not boiling, whisk it into the puréed avocado.

3 Season to taste with salt and pepper. Serve immediately, sprinkled with the cilantro, if using. The soup may be served chilled, if desired.

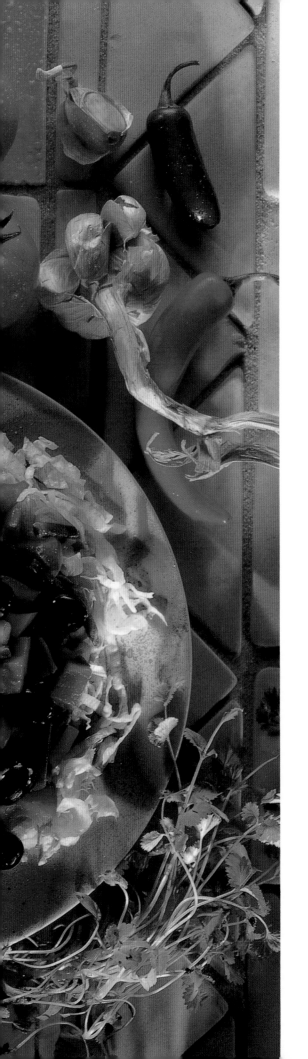

VEGETABLES AND SALADS

Mexico is blessed with a bounty of vegetables. The New World vegetables first cultivated by the Aztec and Maya-Toltec civilizations thousands of years ago include corn, all the peppers (sweet, pungent and hot), tomatoes, common beans like red and black kidney beans, pinto beans, pumpkins, zucchini, chayote (chocho), avocados, potatoes, sweet potatoes, and lima beans from the Inca Empire, now modern Peru and Bolivia. The Spanish Conquistadores brought in European vegetables like cabbage, chick-peas, cucumbers, regional types of onion and garlic, cauliflower, turnips, green peas and eggplant. As a result of the marriage of foods and cooking methods, many new dishes were created, especially salads.

Frijoles

INGREDIENTS

Serves 6 – 8

1¼ – 1½ cups dried red kidney,
    pinto or black beans, rinsed and
    picked over
2 onions, finely chopped
2 garlic cloves, chopped
1 bay leaf
1 or more *serrano* chilies (small fresh
    hot green chilies)
2 tablespoons corn oil
2 tomatoes, peeled, seeded and
    chopped
salt
sprigs of fresh bay leaves, to garnish

—————— COOK'S TIP ——————

In the Yucatán, black haricot beans are
cooked with the Mexican herb *epazote*.

1 Put the beans into a pan and add
cold water to cover by 1 inch.

2 Add half the onion, half the garlic,
the bay leaf and the chili(es). Bring
to a boil and boil vigorously for about
10 minutes. Put the beans and liquid
into a large saucepan, cover and cook
over low heat for 30 minutes. Add
boiling water if the beans start to
become dry.

3 When the beans begin to wrinkle,
add 1 tablespoon of the corn oil
and cook for another 30 minutes or
until the beans are tender. Add salt to
taste and cook for 30 minutes more,
but do not add any more water.

4 Remove the beans from the heat.
Heat the remaining oil in a small
frying pan and sauté the remaining
onion and garlic until the onion is soft.
Add the tomatoes and cook for a few
minutes more.

5 Spoon 3 tablespoons of the beans
out of the pot or pan and add
them to the tomato mixture. Mash to a
paste. Stir this into the beans to thicken
the liquid. Cook for just long enough
to heat through, if necessary. Serve the
beans in small bowls and garnish with
sprigs of fresh bay leaves.

Peppers Stuffed with Beans

Stuffed peppers are a popular Mexican dish. A special version – *Chiles en Nogada* – is served every year on August 28 to celebrate Independence Day. The green peppers are served with a sauce of fresh walnuts and a garnish of pomegranate seeds to represent the colors of the Mexican flag.

INGREDIENTS

Serves 6

6 large green bell peppers
1 recipe Frijoles Refritos (Refried Beans)
2 eggs, separated
½ teaspoon salt
corn oil, for frying
all-purpose flour, for dusting
½ cup whipping cream
1 cup grated Cheddar cheese
fresh cilantro sprigs, to garnish

1 Roast the peppers over a gas flame or under the broiler, turning occasionally, until the skins have blackened and blistered. Transfer the peppers to a plastic bag, secure the top and let sit for 15 minutes.

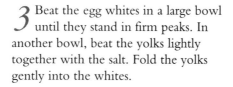

2 Preheat the oven to 350°F. Remove the peppers from the bag. Hold each pepper in turn under cold running water and gently rub off the skins. Slit the peppers down one side and remove the seeds and ribs, taking care not to break the pepper shells. Stuff with the Refried Beans.

3 Beat the egg whites in a large bowl until they stand in firm peaks. In another bowl, beat the yolks lightly together with the salt. Fold the yolks gently into the whites.

4 Pour the corn oil into a large frying pan to a depth of about 1 inch and heat. Spread out the flour in a shallow bowl or dish.

5 Dip the filled peppers in the flour and then in the egg mixture. Fry in batches in the hot oil until golden brown all over. Arrange the peppers in an ovenproof dish. Pour on the cream and sprinkle with the cheese. Bake in the oven for 30 minutes or until the topping is golden brown and the peppers are heated through. Serve at once, garnished with cilantro.

Chopped Zucchini

Calabacitas is an extremely easy recipe to make. If the cooking time seems unduly long, this is because the acid present in the tomatoes slows down the cooking of the zucchini. Use young tender zucchini.

INGREDIENTS

Serves 4
2 tablespoons corn oil
1 pound young zucchini, sliced
1 onion, finely chopped
2 garlic cloves, chopped
1 pound tomatoes, peeled, seeded and chopped
2 drained canned *jalapeño* peppers, rinsed, seeded and chopped
1 tablespoon chopped fresh cilantro
salt
fresh cilantro, to garnish

1 Heat the oil in a flameproof casserole and add all the remaining ingredients, except the salt.

2 Bring to simmering point, cover and cook over low heat for about 30 minutes until the zucchini are tender, checking from time to time that the dish is not drying out. If it is, add a little tomato juice, stock or water.

3 Season with salt and serve the Mexican way as a separate course. Alternatively, serve accompanied by any plainly cooked meat or poultry. Garnish with cilantro.

Refried Beans (Frijoles Refritos)

There is much disagreement about the translation of the term *refrito*. It means, literally, twice fried. Some cooks say this implies that the beans must be really well fried, others that it means twice cooked. However named, *Frijoles Refritos* are delicious.

INGREDIENTS

Serves 6–8
6–8 tablespoons lard or corn oil
1 onion, finely chopped
1 recipe Frijoles (cooked beans)

To garnish
freshly grated Parmesan cheese or crumbled farmer cheese
crisp-fried corn tortillas, cut into quarters

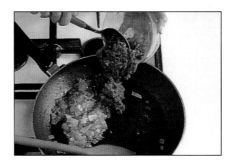 

1 Heat 2 tablespoons of the lard in a large heavy frying pan and sauté the onion until it is soft and starting to turn translucent. Add about 1 cup of the Frijoles (cooked beans).

— COOK'S TIP —

Lard is the traditional (and best-tasting) fat for the beans, but many people prefer to use corn oil. Avoid using olive oil, which is too strongly flavored and distinctive.

2 Mash the beans with the back of a wooden spoon or potato masher, adding more beans and melted lard or oil until all the ingredients are used up and the beans have formed a heavy paste. Use extra lard if necessary.

3 Transfer to a warmed platter, piling the mixture up in a roll. Garnish with the cheese. Spike with the tortilla triangles, placing them at intervals along the length of the roll. Serve as a side dish.

Mushrooms with Chipotle Chilies

INGREDIENTS

Serves 6

4 cups button mushrooms
4 tablespoons olive oil
1 onion, finely chopped
2 garlic cloves, chopped
2 drained canned *chipotle* chilies, rinsed
 and sliced
salt
chopped fresh cilantro, to garnish

COOK'S TIP

Never wash mushrooms, as they quickly absorb water. Wipe them with a paper towel or a clean, damp cloth.

1 Wipe the mushrooms gently and carefully with kitchen paper. Heat the olive oil in a large heavy frying pan and add the mushrooms, onion, garlic, and sliced *chipotles*. Stir to coat the vegetables in oil.

2 Fry the mixture over medium heat for 6–8 minutes, stirring from time to time, until the onions and mushrooms are tender. Season to taste with salt and serve on small individual plates, sprinkled with a little chopped fresh cilantro.

Shrimp Salad

Salads in Mexico are usually served with the main course instead of green vegetables. Salads containing meat or seafood are served as a separate course, since they are very satisfying.

INGREDIENTS

Serves 4

1 iceberg lettuce, separated into leaves,
 or assorted lettuce leaves
¼ cup mayonnaise
¼ cup sour cream
12 ounces cooked shrimp,
 chopped
½ cup chopped cooked green beans
½ cup chopped cooked carrots
½ cucumber, about 4 ounces
 chopped
2 hard-cooked eggs, coarsely
 chopped
1 drained pickled *jalapeño* pepper,
 seeded and chopped
salt

1 Line a large salad bowl or platter with the lettuce leaves. Stir together the mayonnaise and sour cream in a small bowl and set aside.

2 Combine the shrimp, beans, carrot, cucumber, eggs and *jalapeño* in a separate bowl. Season with salt.

3 Add the mayonnaise and sour cream mixture to the shrimp, folding it in very gently so that all the ingredients are well mixed and coated with the dressing. Pile the mixture into the lined salad bowl or arrange attractively on the platter and serve.

Green Lima Beans in Sauce

A tasty dish of lima beans with a tomato and chili sauce.

INGREDIENTS

Serves 4

1 pound lima or fava beans, thawed
   if frozen
2 tablespoons olive oil
1 onion, finely chopped
2 garlic cloves, chopped
12 ounces tomatoes, peeled, seeded
   and chopped
1 or 2 drained canned *jalapeño* peppers,
   seeded and chopped
salt
chopped fresh cilantro sprigs,
   to garnish

1 Cook the beans in a saucepan of boiling water for 15–20 minutes, until tender. Drain and keep hot, to one side, in the covered saucepan.

2 Heat the olive oil in a frying pan and sauté the onion and garlic until the onion is soft but not brown. Add the tomatoes and cook until the mixture is thick and flavorful.

3 Add the *jalapeños* and cook for 1–2 minutes. Season with salt.

4 Pour the mixture over the reserved beans and check that they are hot. If not, return everything to the frying pan and cook over low heat just long enough to heat through. Put into a warm serving dish, garnish with cilantro and serve.

Green Bean and Sweet Red Pepper Salad

INGREDIENTS

Serves 4

12 ounces cooked green beans, quartered
2 red peppers, seeded and chopped
2 scallions (white and green parts), chopped
1 or more drained pickled *serrano* chilies, well rinsed, seeded and chopped
1 iceberg lettuce, coarsely shredded, or mixed salad leaves
olives, to garnish

For the dressing

3 tablespoons red wine vinegar
9 tablespoons olive oil
salt and freshly ground black pepper

1 Combine the cooked green beans, chopped peppers, chopped scallions and chilies in a salad bowl.

2 Make the salad dressing. Pour the red wine vinegar into a bowl or cup. Add salt and freshly ground black pepper to taste, then gradually whisk in the olive oil until well combined.

3 Pour the salad dressing over the prepared vegetables and toss lightly together to mix and coat thoroughly.

4 Line a large platter with the shredded lettuce leaves and arrange the salad attractively on top. Garnish with the olives and serve.

Avocado and Tomato Salad

INGREDIENTS

Serves 4

2 ripe avocados
2 large beefsteak tomatoes, about
  8 ounces each, peeled and seeded
1 iceberg lettuce, coarsely shredded, or
  mixed salad leaves
2 tablespoons chopped fresh cilantro
salt and freshly ground black pepper

For the dressing
6 tablespoons olive or corn oil
2 tablespoons fresh lemon juice

1 Cut the avocados in half, remove the pits and peel off the skin. Then cut the avocados and tomatoes into equal numbers of lengthwise slices of approximately the same size.

2 Arrange a bed of shredded lettuce on a large platter and place the tomato slices on top. Arrange the avocado slices over the tomato and sprinkle with the cilantro. Season to taste with salt and pepper.

3 Whisk the olive oil and lemon juice together in a bowl or cup until well combined.

4 Pour a little dressing over the salad and serve the rest separately.

> ——— COOK'S TIP ———
>
> To ripen avocados, put them in a brown paper bag and store in a dark place for several days, checking from time to time. They are ready when they yield to a gentle pressure at the stem end.

Chayote Salad

Chayote goes by several different names – chocho, christophine or vegetable pear being the most common. Native to Mexico, they are now widely cultivated in the Caribbean, Southeast Asia and parts of Africa.

INGREDIENTS

Serves 4

2 chayotes, peeled and halved
1 large beefsteak tomato, about
  8 ounces, peeled and cut into
  6 wedges
1 small onion, finely chopped
strips of seeded pickled *jalapeño*
  peppers, to garnish

For the dressing
½ teaspoon Dijon mustard
2 tablespoons mild white vinegar
6 tablespoons olive or corn oil
salt and freshly ground black pepper

1 Leaving the seeds in place, cook the chayotes in a large saucepan of boiling salted water for about 20 minutes or until tender. Drain and set aside to cool. Remove the seeds and set them aside (see Cook's Tip). Cut the flesh into chunks about the same size as the tomato wedges.

2 Make the dressing directly in a salad bowl. Combine the Dijon mustard and the vinegar with salt and pepper to taste. Gradually whisk in the oil until well combined.

3 Put the chayote chunks, tomato wedges and finely chopped onion into a bowl. Add the dressing and toss gently together until well coated.

4 Put in a serving dish, garnish with the chili strips and serve.

> ——— COOK'S TIP ———
>
> The edible seed of the chayote is a very desirable cook's perk.

FISH AND SHELLFISH

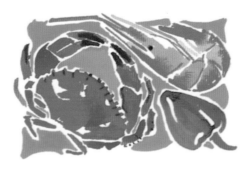

Mexico has an extensive coastline and an abundance of seafood, much of which is available here in good fish markets. The catch includes red snapper, mackerel, sea bass, striped bass and shrimp. Red snapper is used for the nation's most famous dish, Huachinango a la Veracruzana (Red Snapper, Veracruz-style). Another world-renowned dish is Seviche, which may be a Mexican invention, or could have originated in Polynesia. This delectable appetizer consists of fish "cooked" in lime or lemon juice. Thanks to the influence of Spain and Portugal, there are also numerous dishes made with that perennial favorite, dried salt cod. Most of the following fish dishes can be made using fillets of any firm-fleshed, non-oily fish.

Striped Bass in Sauce

This is a typical Mayan dish.

INGREDIENTS

Serves 6

3–3½pounds striped bass or any non-oily white fish, cut into 6 steaks
½ cup corn oil
1 large onion, thinly sliced
2 garlic cloves, chopped
12 ounces tomatoes, sliced
2 drained canned *jalapeño* peppers, rinsed and sliced
flat-leaf parsley, to garnish

For the marinade

4 garlic cloves, crushed
1 teaspoon black peppercorns
1 teaspoon dried oregano
½ teaspoon ground cumin
1 teaspoon ground *achiote* (annatto)
½ teaspoon ground cinnamon
½ cup mild white vinegar
salt

1 Arrange the fish steaks in a single layer in a shallow dish. Make the marinade. Using a pestle, grind the garlic and black peppercorns in a mortar. Add the dried oregano, cumin, *achiote* (annatto) and cinnamon and mix to a paste with the vinegar. Add salt to taste and spread the marinade on both sides of each of the fish steaks. Cover and let sit in a cool place for 1 hour.

2 Select a flameproof dish large enough to hold the fish in a single layer, and pour in enough of the oil to coat the bottom. Arrange the fish in the dish with any remaining marinade.

3 Top the fish with the onion, garlic, tomatoes and chilies and pour the rest of the oil over the top.

4 Cover the dish and cook over low heat on top of the stove for 15–20 minutes, or until the fish is no longer translucent. Serve at once garnished with flat leaf parsley.

Salt Cod in Mild Chili Sauce

INGREDIENTS

Serves 6

2 pounds dried salt cod
1 onion, chopped
2 garlic cloves, chopped
1 fresh green chili, sliced, to garnish

For the sauce

6 dried *ancho* chilies
1 onion, chopped
½ teaspoon dried oregano
½ teaspoon ground coriander
1 *serrano* chili, seeded and chopped
3 tablespoons corn oil
3 cups fish or chicken stock
salt

COOK'S TIP

Dried salt cod is a great favorite in Spain and Portugal and throughout Latin America. Look for it in Spanish and Portuguese markets.

1 Soak the cod in cold water for several hours, depending on how hard and salty it is. Change the water once or twice during soaking.

2 Drain the fish and transfer it to a saucepan. Pour in water to cover. Bring to a gentle simmer and cook for about 15 minutes, until the fish is tender. Drain, reserving the stock. Remove any skin or bones from the fish and cut it into 1½-inch pieces.

3 Make the sauce. Remove the stems and shake out the seeds from the *ancho* chilies. Tear the pods into pieces, put in a bowl of warm water and soak until they are soft.

4 Drain the soaked chilies and put them into a food processor with the onion, oregano, coriander and *serrano* chili. Process to a purée.

5 Heat the oil in a frying pan and cook the purée, stirring, for about 5 minutes. Stir in the fish or chicken stock and simmer for 3–4 minutes.

6 Add the prepared cod and simmer for a few minutes longer to heat the fish through and blend the flavors. Serve garnished with the sliced chili.

Crab with Green Rice

INGREDIENTS

Serves 4

1 cup long-grain rice
4 tablespoons olive oil
10-ounce can tomatillos (Mexican
  green tomatoes)
1 onion, chopped
2 garlic cloves, chopped
2 tablespoons chopped fresh cilantro
about 1½ cups chicken stock
1 pound crab meat, thawed if frozen,
  broken into chunks
salt
chopped fresh cilantro, to garnish
lettuce leaves, to serve

1 Soak the rice in enough hot water to cover for 15 minutes, then drain thoroughly. Heat the oil in a frying pan and sauté the rice over medium heat, stirring until the rice is golden and the oil has been absorbed.

2 Drain the tomatillos, reserving the juice, and put them into a food processor. Add the onion, garlic and cilantro, and process to a purée. Pour into a measuring cup and add the tomatillo juice. Pour in enough stock to make 2 cups. Season the mixture to taste with salt.

3 Place the rice, tomato mixture and crab meat in a shallow pan. Cover and cook over very low heat for about 30 minutes, or until the liquid has been absorbed and the rice is tender. Serve on lettuce leaves, garnished with chopped fresh cilantro.

--- COOK'S TIP ---

Mexican cooks always soak rice in water before cooking it. This seems to pay off, as their rice is always delicious, with every grain separate.

Shrimp with Pumpkin Seed Sauce

INGREDIENTS

Serves 4

1 generous cup *pepitas* (Mexican
  pumpkin seeds)
1 pound raw shrimp, peeled
  and de-veined
1 onion, chopped
1 garlic clove, chopped
2 tablespoons chopped fresh cilantro
8 ounces tomatoes, peeled and
  chopped
1 drained canned *jalapeño* pepper,
  rinsed, seeded and chopped
1 red bell pepper, seeded and chopped
2 tablespoons corn oil
salt
whole cooked shrimp, lemon slices and
  fresh cilantro sprigs, to garnish
rice, to serve

1 Grind the pumpkin seeds finely, shake through a sieve into a bowl and set aside.

2 Cook the shrimp in boiling salted water. As soon as they turn pink, remove with a slotted spoon and set them aside. Reserve the cooking water.

3 Purée the onion, garlic, cilantro, tomatoes, *jalapeño*, bell pepper and pumpkin seeds in a food processor. Heat the oil in a pan, stir and cook the mixture for 5 minutes. Season. Add shrimp water to thin the mixture to a sauce consistency. Heat gently, add the shrimp. Garnish and serve with rice.

Seviche

This makes an excellent appetizer. With the addition of sliced avocado, it could make a light summer lunch for four.

INGREDIENTS

Serves 6

1 pound mackerel fillets, cut into
  ½-inch pieces
1½ cups freshly squeezed lime or
  lemon juice
8 ounces tomatoes, chopped
1 small onion, very finely chopped
2 drained canned *jalapeño* peppers or
  4 *serrano* chilies, rinsed and chopped
4 tablespoons olive oil
½ teaspoon dried oregano
2 tablespoons chopped fresh cilantro
salt and freshly ground black pepper
lemon wedges and fresh cilantro,
  to garnish
stuffed olives, to serve

1 Put the fish into a glass dish and top with the lime juice, making sure that the fish is completely covered. Cover and chill for 6 hours, turning once. The fish will be opaque, "cooked" by the juice.

<table>
<tr><td>—— COOK'S TIP ——</td></tr>
</table>

For a more delicately flavored Seviche, use a white fish such as sole.

2 When the fish is opaque, lift it out of the juice and set it aside.

3 Combine the tomatoes, onion, peppers or chilies, olive oil, oregano and cilantro in a bowl. Add salt and pepper to taste, then pour in the reserved juice from the mackerel. Mix well and pour over the fish.

4 Cover the dish and return the seviche to the fridge for about an hour to allow the flavors to blend. Seviche should not be served too cold. Allow it to stand at room temperature for 15 minutes before serving. Garnish with lemon wedges and cilantro sprigs, and serve with stuffed olives sprinkled with chopped cilantro.

Red Snapper with Cilantro

As it is caught in the Gulf of Mexico, red snapper is used in this dish, but you can use any fillets of firm white fish instead.

INGREDIENTS

Serves 4

2 pounds red snapper fillets or other whitefish fillets
6 tablespoons lime or lemon juice
4 tablespoons olive oil
1 onion, finely chopped
1 cup fresh cilantro, finely chopped
2 drained canned *jalapeño* peppers, rinsed, seeded and sliced
salt and freshly ground black pepper
tomato rice, to serve

1 Place the fish in a shallow dish. Season with salt and pepper and drizzle the lime juice over. Cover and set aside for 15 minutes.

2 Preheat the oven to 350°F. Heat all but 1 tablespoon of the oil in a heavy frying pan and sauté the onion until it is soft.

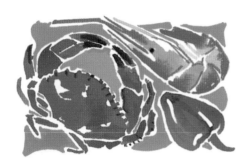

3 Use the reserved oil to thinly coat the bottom of an ovenproof dish which is just large enough to hold the fish fillets in a single layer. Arrange the fish in the dish and pour over any of the remaining marinating liquid. Top with the sautéed onion and the oil from the pan.

4 Sprinkle with the cilantro and chilies. Bake for 20–25 minutes, or until the fish is no longer translucent. Serve with tomato rice.

COOK'S TIP

This may seem like a lot of cilantro but it cooks down with the chilies, onion and pan juices to make a delicious sauce.

Shrimp in Sauce

This colorful dish is called *Camarones en Salsa* in Mexico – serve it with rice, if you like.

INGREDIENTS

Serves 4
4 tablespoons olive or corn oil
1 red bell pepper, seeded and chopped
2 large scallions (white and green parts), chopped
2 garlic cloves, chopped
1 pound tomatoes, peeled, seeded and chopped
4 tablespoons chopped fresh cilantro
a little chicken stock
1 pound raw or cooked shrimp, thawed if frozen, peeled and de-veined
salt and freshly ground black pepper
fresh cilantro, for garnish

1 Heat the oil in a flameproof casserole and sauté the pepper, scallions and garlic until the pepper is soft. Add the tomatoes and simmer for about 10 minutes or until the mixture is thick and flavorful.

2 Add the cilantro and salt and pepper to taste. If the sauce is very thick, thin with chicken stock.

3 Add the shrimp and cook for 2–3 minutes, depending on the size, until they turn pink. Be very careful not to overcook the shrimp; they toughen very quickly. Serve at once, with rice if desired, and garnish with fresh cilantro.

Fish in Parsley Sauce

INGREDIENTS

Serves 6
10-ounce can tomatillos (Mexican green tomatoes)
1 onion, finely chopped
2 garlic cloves, chopped
1 cup flat-leaf parsley, finely chopped
4 tablespoons olive oil
6 firm-fleshed whitefish fillets
salt and freshly ground black pepper

To garnish
drained canned *serrano* chilies, seeded, rinsed and shredded
sliced black olives

COOK'S TIP

Flat-leaf or Italian parsley has much more flavor than curly parsley. Keep the curly variety for use as a decoration and use the flat leaf parsley in cooking.

1 Drain the tomatillos, reserving the liquid. Mash them in a bowl with the onion, garlic and parsley. Season with salt and pepper and set aside.

2 Heat the oil in a large frying pan and sauté the fish fillets until they are golden on both sides. Using a spatula, transfer the fillets to a warmed serving dish, cover and keep hot.

3 Heat the oil remaining in the pan and add the tomatillo mixture. Cook over moderate heat, stirring from time to time, until the sauce is well blended and has the consistency of light cream. If it is too thick, add a little of the reserved tomatillo juice. Season to taste with salt and pepper.

4 Pour the sauce over the fish fillets, garnish with the *serrano* chilies and black olives and serve.

Pickled Fish (Pescado en Escabeche)

INGREDIENTS

Serves 4

2 pounds whitefish fillets
4 tablespoons freshly squeezed lime or
    lemon juice
1¼ cups olive or corn oil
2 whole cloves
6 peppercorns
2 garlic cloves
½ teaspoon ground cumin
½ teaspoon dried oregano
2 bay leaves
1 drained canned *jalapeño* pepper,
    seeded, and cut into strips
1 onion, thinly sliced
1 cup white wine vinegar
1 cup olive or corn oil
salt

To garnish

lettuce leaves
green olives

1 Cut the fish fillets into eight pieces and arrange them in a single layer in a shallow dish. Drizzle with the lime juice. Cover and marinate for 15 minutes, turning the fillets once.

2 Lift out the fillets with a spatula, pat dry with paper towels and season with salt. Heat 4 tablespoons of the oil in a frying pan and sauté the fish until lightly golden brown. Transfer to a platter and set aside.

3 Combine the cloves, peppercorns, garlic, cumin, oregano, bay leaves, chili and vinegar in a pan. Bring to a boil, then simmer for 3–4 minutes.

4 Add the remaining oil, and bring to a simmer. Pour over the fish. Cool, cover and chill for 24 hours. To serve, lift out the fillets with a spatula and arrange on a serving dish. Garnish with lettuce and olives.

--- COOK'S TIP ---

To make the dish special, add an elaborate garnish of radishes, capers and chili strips.

Red Snapper, Veracruz-style

This is Mexico's best-known fish dish. In Veracruz, red snapper is always used but fillets of any firm-fleshed white fish can be substituted successfully.

INGREDIENTS

Serves 4

4 large red snapper fillets
2 tablespoons freshly squeezed lime or lemon juice
½ cup olive oil
1 onion, finely chopped
2 garlic cloves, chopped
1½ pounds tomatoes, peeled and chopped
1 bay leaf, plus a few sprigs for garnish
¼ teaspoon dried oregano
2 tablespoons large capers, plus extra to serve (optional)
16 pitted green olives, halved
2 drained canned *jalapeño* peppers, seeded and cut into strips
butter, for frying
3 slices firm white bread, cut into triangles
salt and freshly ground black pepper

1 Arrange the fish fillets in a single layer in a shallow dish. Season with salt and pepper, drizzle with the lime juice and set aside.

2 Heat the oil in a large frying pan and sauté the onion and garlic until the onion is soft. Add the tomatoes and cook for about 10 minutes until the mixture is thick and flavorful. Stir the mixture from time to time.

3 Stir in the bay leaf, oregano, capers, olives and chilies. Add the fish and cook over very low heat for about 10 minutes or until tender.

— COOK'S TIP —

This dish can also be made with a whole red snapper, weighing about 3–3½ pounds. Bake together with the sauce, in a preheated oven at 325°F. Allow 10 minutes cooking time for every 1 inch of the fish's thickness.

4 While the fish is cooking, heat the butter in a small frying pan and sauté the bread triangles until they are golden brown on both sides.

5 Transfer the fish to a heated platter, pour over the sauce and surround with the fried bread triangles. Garnish with bay leaves and serve with extra capers, if you like.

MEAT
AND
POULTRY

Wild boar roamed Mexico before the Conquest, as did deer and several animals related to the rabbit. The native inhabitants had domesticated the turkey, and also cooked dove, quail and pheasant (the curassow), but it took the Spanish Conquistadores to introduce the domestic hen. The Spaniards also brought cattle, sheep, goats and pigs. Apart from the great national festive dish, Mole Poblano de Guajolote, made with turkey, most dishes were creative combinations of foods and cooking methods from both the Old and New Worlds.

Pheasant in Green Pipian Sauce

INGREDIENTS

Serves 4

2 oven-ready pheasants
2 tablespoons corn oil
1 generous cup *pepitas* (Mexican pumpkin seeds)
1 tablespoon *achiote* (annatto) seeds
1 onion, finely chopped
2 garlic cloves, chopped
10-ounce can tomatillos (Mexican green tomatoes)
2 cups chicken stock
salt and freshly ground black pepper
fresh cilantro, to garnish

--- COOK'S TIP ---

Achiote is a typical ingredient in the Yucatán. It adds a subtle flavor and an orange-red color. There is no substitute. Look for it in Latin American markets.

1 Preheat the oven to 350°F. Using a large sharp knife or poultry shears, cut the pheasants in half lengthwise and season well with salt and pepper. Heat the oil in a large frying pan and sauté the pieces until lightly brown on all sides. Lift out, drain and arrange, skin-side up, in a roasting pan large enough to hold them comfortably in one layer. Set aside.

2 Grind the *pepitas* finely in a nut grinder or a food processor. Shake through a sieve into a bowl. Grind the *achiote* seeds, add them to the bowl and set aside.

3 Put the onion, garlic, tomatillos and their juice into a food processor and purée. Put in a saucepan.

4 Add the *pepita* mixture, stir in the stock and simmer over very low heat for 10 minutes. Do not let the mixture boil, or it will separate. Cool.

5 Pour sauce over the pheasant halves. Bake for 40 minutes, or until tender, basting occasionally with the sauce. Garnish with cilantro.

Chicken in Green Almond Sauce

INGREDIENTS

Serves 6

3 – 3½ pounds chicken, cut into serving
   pieces
2 cups chicken stock
1 onion, chopped
1 garlic clove, chopped
2 cups fresh cilantro, coarsely chopped
1 green bell pepper, seeded and
   chopped
1 *jalapeño* pepper, seeded and chopped
1 can (10 ounces) tomatillos (Mexican
   green tomatoes)
1 cup ground almonds
2 tablespoons corn oil
salt
fresh cilantro, to garnish
rice, to serve

1 Put the chicken pieces into a
flameproof casserole or shallow
pan. Pour in the stock, bring to a
simmer, cover and cook for about 45
minutes, until tender. Drain the stock
into a measuring cup and set aside.

2 Put the onion, garlic, cilantro, bell
pepper, *jalapeño*, tomatillos and
their juice and the almonds in a food
processor. Purée fairly coarsely.

3 Heat the oil in a frying pan, add
the almond mixture and cook over
low heat, stirring with a wooden
spoon, for 3 – 4 minutes. Scrape into
the casserole with the chicken.

— COOK'S TIP —

If the the sauce looks a little pale, add 2
or 3 outer leaves of dark green romaine lettuce. Cut out the central veins, chop the
leaves and add to the food processor with
the other ingredients. This will brighten
the color without altering the flavor.

4 Add water to the stock to make
2 cups, if necessary. Stir it into
the casserole. Mix gently and simmer
just long enough to blend the flavors
and heat the chicken pieces through.
Add salt to taste. Serve the chicken at
once, garnished with cilantro and
accompanied by rice.

Mole Poblano de Guajolote

Mole Poblano de Guajolote is *the* great festive dish of Mexico. It is served at any special occasion, be it a birthday, wedding, or family get-together. Rice, beans, tortillas and guacamole are the traditional accompaniments.

INGREDIENTS

Serves 6–8

6–8 pounds turkey, cut into
    serving pieces
1 onion, chopped
1 garlic clove, chopped
salt
6 tablespoons lard or corn oil
fresh cilantro and 2 tablespoons toasted
    sesame seeds, to garnish

For the sauce

6 dried *ancho* chilies
4 dried *pasilla* chilies
4 dried *mulato* chilies
1 drained canned *chipotle* chili, seeded
    and chopped (optional)
2 onions, chopped
2 garlic cloves, chopped
1 pound tomatoes, peeled
    and chopped
1 stale tortilla, torn into pieces
1/3 cup raisins
1 cup ground almonds
3 tablespoons sesame seeds, ground
1/2 tsp coriander seeds, ground
1 teaspoon ground cinnamon
1/2 teaspoon ground anise
1/4 teaspoon ground black peppercorns
4 tablespoons lard or corn oil
1 1/2 ounces unsweetened chocolate,
    broken into squares
1 tablespoon sugar
salt and freshly ground pepper

COOK'S TIP

Roasting the dried chilies lightly, taking care not to burn them, brings out the flavor and is worth the extra effort.

---

1 Put the turkey pieces into a saucepan or flameproof casserole large enough to hold them in one layer comfortably. Add the onion and garlic, and enough cold water to cover. Season with salt, bring to a gentle simmer, cover and cook for about 1 hour or until the turkey is tender.

2 Meanwhile, put the *ancho, pasilla* and *mulato* chilies in a dry frying pan over gentle heat and roast them for a few minutes, shaking the pan frequently. Remove the stems and shake out the seeds. Tear the pods into pieces and put these into a small bowl. Add sufficient warm water to just cover and soak, turning from time to time, for 30 minutes, or until soft.

3 Lift out the turkey pieces and pat dry with paper towels. Reserve the stock in a measuring jug. Heat the lard in a large heavy frying pan and sauté the turkey pieces until lightly browned all over. Transfer to a plate and set aside. Reserve any oil left in the frying pan.

4 Transfer the chilies, along with the water in which they have been soaked, into a food processor. Add the *chipotle* chili, if using, with the onions, garlic, tomatoes, tortilla, raisins, ground almonds and spices. Process to a purée. Do this in batches, if necessary.

5 Add the lard to the fat remaining in the frying pan used for sautéing the turkey. Heat the mixture, then add the chili and spice paste. Cook, stirring, for 5 minutes.

6 Transfer the mixture to the pan or casserole in which the turkey was originally cooked. Stir in 2 cups of the turkey stock (make up the difference with water if necessary). Add the chocolate and season with salt and pepper. Cook over low heat until the chocolate has melted. Stir in the sugar. Add the turkey and more stock if needed. Cover the pan and simmer very gently for 30 minutes. Serve, garnished with fresh cilantro and sprinkled with the sesame seeds.

Smoked Beef Tongue with Tomatillos

Tomatillos have a delicious, distinctive flavor and color.

INGREDIENTS

Serves 6–8

1 smoked beef tongue, about 5 pounds
3 tablespoons corn oil
2 onions, finely chopped
2 garlic cloves, chopped
3 or 4 drained pickled *serrano* or
   jalapeño peppers, seeded and chopped
2 tablespoons chopped fresh cilantro
2 x 10-ounce cans tomatillos (Mexican
   green tomatoes)
salt and freshly ground pepper
fresh cilantro, to garnish
small new potatoes, to serve

1 Thoroughly wash the tongue and put it into a large saucepan. Cover with cold water and bring to a boil. Remove any scum that rises to the surface. Lower the heat and simmer, covered, for 3–4 hours, until tender. Allow the tongue to cool in the stock.

2 Lift out the tongue when it is cool enough to handle, reserving the stock. Peel the skin from the tongue and trim the root end and discard. Cut the tongue into fairly thick slices and place these in a flameproof casserole.

3 Heat the oil in a large frying pan and sauté the onions and garlic with the chilies until the onion is tender. Add the cilantro, the tomatillos (with the can juices) and salt and pepper to taste. Stir to mix and pour over the tongue, adding a little reserved stock if the mixture is thick.

4 Cover the pan with foil or a lid and cook over a moderate heat for about 15 minutes, until hot. Serve at once, garnished with cilantro sprigs and accompanied by new potatoes sprinkled with chopped cilantro.

COOK'S TIP

Fresh lamb's tongues can be used – they only need to be cooked for 45–60 minutes.

Beef with Cactus Pieces

Nopalitos – edible cactus chunks – are used widely in Mexico, and are the basis of several salads, soups and casseroles.

INGREDIENTS

Serves 6

2 pounds braising beef, cut into
  2-inch cubes
2 tablespoons corn oil
1 onion, finely chopped
2 garlic cloves, chopped
1 or 2 *jalapeño* peppers, seeded and
  chopped
1 can (4 ounces) *nopalitos* (cactus
  pieces), rinsed and drained
2 cans (10 ounces each) tomatillos
  (Mexican green tomatoes)
½ cup chopped fresh cilantro
beef stock (optional)
salt and freshly ground black pepper
chopped fresh cilantro, to garnish

1 Pat the beef cubes dry with paper towels. Heat the oil in a frying pan and sauté the beef cubes a few at a time, until browned all over. Using a slotted spoon, transfer the beef cubes to a flameproof casserole or pan.

2 Add the onion and garlic to the oil remaining in the frying pan and sauté until the onion is tender. Add more oil, if necessary. Add the onions and garlic to the casserole, along with the *jalapeños*.

3 Add the *nopalitos* and tomatillos, with the can juices, to the casserole. Stir in the cilantro until well mixed. If more liquid is needed to cover the beef, stir in as much stock as needed. Season with salt and pepper.

4 Bring to a slow simmer, cover and cook over low heat for about 2½ hours, or until the beef is very tender. Serve sprinkled with the chopped cilantro.

COOK'S TIP

Tomatillos (Mexican green tomatoes) are not to be confused with ordinary green, unripe, tomatoes. Look for them canned, in most supermarkets. Fresh tomatillos are also widely available.

Lamb Stew

This stew is known as *Estofado de Carnero* in Mexico. The recipe for this dish has an interesting mix of chilies – the mild, full-flavored *ancho,* and the piquante *jalapeño,* which gives extra bite. The heat of the chilies is mellowed by the addition of ground cinnamon and cloves. Boneless neck fillet is very good for this dish; it is lean, tender, flavorful and inexpensive.

INGREDIENTS

Serves 4
3 dried *ancho* chilies
2 tablespoons olive oil
1 *jalapeño* pepper, seeded and chopped
1 onion, finely chopped
2 garlic cloves, chopped
1 pound tomatoes, peeled and chopped
1/3 cup raisins
1/4 teaspoon ground cinnamon
1/4 teaspoon ground cloves
2 pounds boneless lamb, cut into 2-inch cubes
1 cup lamb stock or water
salt and freshly ground black pepper
a few sprigs fresh cilantro, to garnish
cilantro rice, to serve

1 Roast the *ancho* chilies lightly in a dry frying pan over gentle heat to bring out the flavor.

2 Remove the stems, shake out the seeds, tear the pods into pieces, then put them into a bowl. Pour in enough warm water to just cover. Set aside to soak for 30 minutes.

3 Heat the olive oil in a frying pan and sauté the *jalapeño* together with the onion and garlic until the onion is tender.

4 Add the chopped tomatoes to the pan and cook until the mixture is thick and well blended. Stir in the raisins, ground cinnamon and cloves, and season to taste with salt and ground black pepper. Transfer the mixture to a flameproof casserole.

5 Place the *ancho* chilies and their soaking water in a food processor and process to a smooth purée. Add the chili pureé to the tomato mixture in the casserole.

6 Add the lamb to the casserole, stir to mix and pour in enough of the lamb stock to just cover the meat.

7 Bring to a simmer, then cover the casserole and cook over low heat for about 2 hours or until the lamb is tender. Garnish with fresh cilantro and serve with cilantro rice.

COOK'S TIP

To make cilantro rice, simply heat 2 tablespoons corn oil in a large frying pan and gently cook 1 finely chopped onion for about 8 minutes, or until soft but not brown. Add enough cooked long-grain rice to serve four, and stir gently over medium-low heat until heated through. Sprinkle with 2–3 tablespoons chopped fresh cilantro and stir in thoroughly.

Albondigas

Mexican cooks use twice-ground beef and pork in these meatballs.

INGREDIENTS

Serves 4

8 ounces lean ground beef
8 ounces ground pork
1 cup fresh white breadcrumbs
1 onion, finely chopped
½ teaspoon dried oregano or
    ground cumin
salt and freshly ground black pepper
1 egg, lightly beaten
milk (optional)
corn oil, for frying
oregano leaves, to garnish

For the sauce

beef stock
1 *chipotle* chili, seeded and chopped
1 onion, finely chopped
2 garlic cloves, crushed
8 ounces tomatoes, peeled, seeded and
    finely chopped

1 Put the beef and pork through a grinder or process in a food processor so that the mixture is very finely ground. Place it in a bowl and add the breadcrumbs, onion and oregano or cumin. Season with salt and pepper and stir in the egg.

--- COOK'S TIP ---

The meat balls can be simply poached in beef stock, if you prefer. Alternatively, you can use fresh tomato sauce or salsa, thinned down as required with beef stock.

2 Knead thoroughly with clean hands to make a smooth mixture, adding a little milk if necessary. Shape the mixture into 1½-inch balls.

3 Heat ½ inch oil in a frying pan and fry the balls for 5 minutes, turning occasionally, until browned.

4 Put the meatballs into a shallow pan or flameproof casserole and add beef stock to cover. Add the remaining ingredients and bring to a boil. Simmer for about 30 minutes. Using a slotted spoon, transfer the meatballs to a serving dish. Press the sauce through a sieve, then spoon it over the meatballs. Serve at once, garnished with oregano leaves.

Pork with Pineapple

INGREDIENTS

Serves 6

2 tablespoons corn oil
2 pounds boneless pork shoulder
  or loin, cut into 2-inch cubes
1 onion, finely chopped
1 large red bell pepper, seeded
  and finely chopped
1 or more *jalapeño* peppers, seeded and
  finely chopped
1 pound fresh pineapple chunks
8 fresh mint leaves, chopped
1 cup chicken stock
salt and freshly ground black pepper
fresh mint sprig, to garnish
rice, to serve

1 Heat the oil in a large frying pan
and sauté the pork cubes in batches
until lightly browned. Transfer the
pork to a flameproof casserole, leaving
the oil behind in the pan.

2 Add the onion, red pepper and the
jalapeño to the oil remaining in the
pan. Sauté until the onion is tender,
then add to the casserole with the
pineapple. Stir to combine.

3 Add the mint, then cover and
simmer gently for about 2 hours,
or until the pork is tender. Garnish
with fresh mint and serve with rice.

───── COOK'S TIP ─────

If fresh pineapple is not available, use
pineapple canned in its own juice.

Veal in Nut Sauce

INGREDIENTS

Serves 6

3 – 3½ pounds boneless veal, cut into
2-inch cubes
2 onions, finely chopped
1 garlic clove, crushed
½ teaspoon dried thyme
½ teaspoon dried oregano
1½ cups chicken stock
¾ cup very finely ground almonds,
pecans or peanuts
¾ cup sour cream
fresh oregano, to garnish
rice, to serve

— COOK'S TIP —

Choose domestically raised red veal if you can. It is naturally raised and widely thought to have the best flavor.

1 Put the cubes of veal, finely chopped onions, crushed garlic, thyme, oregano and chicken stock into a large flameproof casserole. Bring to a gentle boil. Cover tightly and simmer over low heat for about 2 hours or until the veal is cooked and tender.

2 Put the ground nuts in a food processor. Add ½ cup of the veal sauce and process for a few seconds until smooth. Press through a sieve into the casserole.

3 Stir in the sour cream and heat through gently, without boiling. Serve at once with rice, if desired.

Picadillo

Serve as a main dish with rice, or use to stuff peppers or fill tacos.

INGREDIENTS

Serves 6

2 tablespoons olive or corn oil
2 pounds ground beef
1 onion, finely chopped
2 garlic cloves, chopped
2 apples
1 pound tomatoes, peeled, seeded and
chopped
2 or 3 drained pickled *jalapeño* peppers,
seeded and chopped
scant ½ cup raisins
¼ teaspoon ground cinnamon
¼ teaspoon ground cumin
salt and freshly ground black pepper
tortilla chips, to serve

To garnish

1 tablespoon butter
¼ cup slivered almonds

1 Heat the oil in a large frying pan, add the beef, onion and garlic and fry, stirring occasionally, until the beef is brown and the onion is tender.

2 Peel, core and chop the apples. Add them to the pan with all the remaining ingredients, except the almonds. Cook, uncovered, for 20 – 25 minutes, stirring occasionally.

3 Just before serving, make the garnish by melting the butter in a small frying pan and sautéing the almonds until golden brown. Serve the Picadillo topped with the almonds and accompanied by the tortilla chips.

DESSERTS

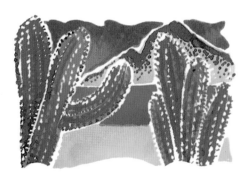

Until the Conquest, fresh fruit was the principal dessert in Mexico, except for sweet tamales. Once the Spanish arrived, bringing with them wheat flour, milk, butter, eggs and sugar, the picture changed and cooks made more elaborate desserts. Some of these combined New and Old World ingredients, while others reflected the Moorish influence in Spanish cuisine. It was the Moors who introduced rice to the Spanish mainland, and with it an enduring favorite, Arroz con Leche, *a rice pudding enriched with raisins, cinnamon, sherry and almonds. Other sweet imports included* flan *(caramel custard) and* buñuelos, *easy-to-make fritters that are absolutely delicious.*

King's Day Bread

January 6, the day the Three Kings brought gifts to the infant Jesus, is a traditional gift-giving day in Mexico, and this iced bread is served.

INGREDIENTS

Serves 8

2 teaspoons active dry yeast
½ cup lukewarm water
2½ cups all-purpose flour
½ teaspoon salt
¼ cup granulated sugar
2 eggs, well beaten
4 egg yolks, slightly beaten
½ cup unsalted butter, softened
2 cups mixed chopped crystallized
 fruit and peel
melted butter, for glazing
1⅓ cups confectioners' sugar, sifted
2 tablespoons light cream
candied cherries, halved, to decorate

1 Sprinkle the yeast over the water, stir and leave for about 5 minutes, or until the mixture is frothy.

2 Put 1¼ cups of the flour in a mixing bowl. Add the salt, sugar, eggs, egg yolks, butter and yeast. Mix well. Put 1¼ cups of the crystallized fruit and peel and ¼ cup of the flour into a bowl and toss to coat. Add to the yeast mixture with the rest of the flour. Beat well with a wooden spoon to make a soft but not sticky dough.

3 Turn out the dough onto a lightly floured board. Knead until smooth.

4 Shape the dough into a ring, place on a greased baking sheet, cover lightly with a cloth and leave in a warm, draft-free place for up to 2 hours, or until it has doubled in size.

5 Preheat the oven to 350°F. Brush the ring with melted butter and bake for 30 minutes. Remove from the oven and cool.

6 In a bowl, mix the confectioners' sugar with the cream. Drizzle the icing over the ring. Decorate with the remaining crystallized fruit and peel and the candied cherries.

Almond Cookies

INGREDIENTS

Makes about 24

1 cup all–purpose flour, sifted
1⅓ cups confectioners' sugar
¼ teaspoon salt
½ cup almonds, finely chopped
½ teaspoon vanilla extract
½ cup unsalted butter, at room
    temperature
confectioners' sugar, for dusting

COOK'S TIP

The cookies can be varied by substituting walnuts, peanuts or pecans, or by adding spices of your choice.

1 Preheat the oven to 350°F. Combine the flour, sugar, salt and almonds in a bowl, mixing well. Stir in the vanilla extract.

2 Using your fingertips, work the butter into the mixture to make a dough. Form it into a ball.

3 Roll out the dough on a lightly floured surface to a thickness of ⅛ inch. Using a round cookie cutter, stamp out into about 24 cookies, re-rolling the trimmings as necessary.

4 Transfer the cookies to baking sheets and bake for 30 minutes, or until they are delicately browned.

5 Cool on wire racks and dust thickly with confectioners' sugar. Store in a tightly closed can or jar.

Churros

INGREDIENTS

Makes about 24
1 cup water
1 tablespoon granulated sugar,
  plus extra for dusting
½ teaspoon salt
1½ cups all-purpose flour
1 large egg
½ lime or lemon
oil for frying

—— COOK'S TIP ——

You can use a funnel to shape the churros.
Close the end with a finger, add the batter,
then release into the oil in small columns.

1 Bring the water, sugar and salt to a
boil. Remove from the heat and
beat in the flour until smooth.

2 Beat in the egg, using a wooden
spoon, until the mixture is smooth
and satiny. Set the batter aside.

3 Pour the oil into a deep-frying pan
to a depth of about 2 inches. Add
the lime half, then heat the oil to
375°F. Test the oil by dropping in a
cube of day-old bread; it should brown
in 30–60 seconds.

4 Pour the batter into a pastry bag
fitted with a fluted nozzle. Pipe
3-inch strips of batter and add to the
oil, a few at a time. Fry for 3–4
minutes, or until golden brown.

5 Using a slotted spoon, remove the
churros from the pan and drain on
paper towels. Roll the hot churros in
granulated sugar before serving.

Sopaipillas

INGREDIENTS

Makes about 30
2 cups all-purpose flour, sifted
1 tablespoon baking powder
1 teaspoon salt
2 tablespoons lard or margarine
¾ cup water
corn oil, for deep frying
syrup or honey, to serve

—— COOK'S TIP ——

Use your imagination when deciding what
to serve with the puffs. Sprinkle them with
cinnamon and sugar, or syrup flavored with
rum. The fat little pillows could even be
served plain, as they taste delicious.

1 Put the flour, baking powder and
salt into a large bowl. Lightly rub
in the lard or margarine, using your
fingertips, until the mixture resembles
coarse breadcrumbs.

2 Gradually stir in the water, using a
fork, until the mixture clumps
together to form a soft dough.

3 Shape the dough into a ball, then
turn out onto a lightly floured
surface and knead very gently until
smooth. Roll out thinly to a rectangle
measuring about 15 x 18 inches. Using
a sharp knife, carefully cut into about
thirty 3-inch squares. For a decorative
edge, you could use a pastry wheel to
cut out the squares.

4 Heat the oil to 375°F, or until a
cube of day-old bread browns in
30–60 seconds.

5 Fry the puffs, a few at a time, in
the oil. As they brown and puff
up, turn over to cook the other side.
Remove with a slotted spoon and drain
on paper towels. It is important that
the temperature of the oil remains
constant during the cooking process.
Serve warm, with syrup or any sauce
of your choice.

Caramel Custard

This is a classic dessert in Mexico where it is known simply as *flan*.

INGREDIENTS

Serves 6

1¼ cups granulated sugar
4 cups milk
6 eggs, lightly beaten
1 teaspoon vanilla extract
pinch of salt

1 Preheat the oven to 350°F. To make the caramel, put ½ cup of the sugar into a small heavy saucepan. Heat, stirring constantly, until the sugar melts. Warm six ramekins by rinsing them in hot water and drying them quickly. Continue to heat the sugar syrup, without stirring, until it turns a deep golden color. Remove the pan from the heat.

2 Pour some of the caramel into a ramekin and turn it so it coats the bottom and sides. As soon as the caramel sets, turn the ramekin upside down on a baking sheet. Coat the remaining ramekins in the same way.

COOK'S TIP

Vary the flavor by adding a little ground cinnamon, cocoa or rum instead of vanilla.

---

3 Scald the milk by heating it in a saucepan to just below boiling point. Pour into a bowl and cool.

4 Put the eggs into a bowl and gradually beat in the remaining sugar. Add the cooled milk, vanilla extract and salt. Mix together well.

5 Strain the egg mixture into the ramekins and put them into a roasting pan filled with enough hot water to come halfway up the sides of the ramekins.

6 Bake for about 40 minutes or until a knife inserted in the center of the custard comes out clean.

7 Cool the custards, then chill for several hours in the fridge.

8 Wet a non-serrated knife and run it between the custard and the side of the ramekin. Put a plate upside down over the ramekin and invert it quickly. The flan will slide out easily.

Rice Pudding

Rice pudding is popular all over the world and is always different. This version – *Arroz con Leche* – is light, attractive and very easy to make.

INGREDIENTS

Serves 4

½ cup raisins
½ cup short-grain rice
1-inch strip lime or lemon peel
1 cup water
2 cups milk
1 cup granulated sugar
¼ teaspoon salt
1-inch cinnamon stick
2 egg yolks, well beaten
1 tablespoon unsalted
  butter, cubed
toasted sliced almonds, to decorate
segments of peeled fresh oranges,
  to serve

COOK'S TIP

It is essential to use short-grain rice for this pudding. It is sometimes sold in bulk or packaged with the name pudding rice.

1 Put the raisins into a small bowl. Cover with warm water and set aside to soak. Put the rice into a saucepan together with the lime or lemon peel and water. Bring slowly to a boil and then lower the heat. Cover the pan and simmer very gently for about 20 minutes, or until all the water has been absorbed.

2 Remove the peel from the rice and discard it. Add the milk, sugar, salt and cinnamon and cook, stirring, over very low heat until all the milk has been absorbed. Do not cover the pan.

3 Discard the cinnamon stick. Add the egg yolks and butter, and cook stirring constantly, until the butter has melted and the pudding is rich and creamy. Drain the raisins well and stir them into the rice. Cook the pudding for a few minutes longer.

4 Pour the rice into a dish and cool. Serve with the orange segments, decorated with the almonds.

Pumpkin in Brown Sugar

INGREDIENTS

Serves 4

2 pounds pumpkin,
  cut into wedges
2 cups dark brown sugar
½ cup water

1 Scrape the seeds out of the pumpkin wedges. Pack the wedges firmly together in a heavy flameproof casserole.

2 Divide the sugar among the pumpkin pieces, packing it into the hollows that contained the seeds.

3 Pour the water carefully into the the casserole to cover the bottom and prevent the pumpkin from burning. Take care not to dislodge the sugar when pouring in the water.

--- COOK'S TIP ---

The best pumpkin for this recipe is the classic orange-fleshed variety used for jack-o'-lanterns. Choose one that will fit neatly into your casserole when cut.

4 Cover and cook over low heat, checking the water level frequently, until the pumpkin is tender and the sugar has dissolved in the liquid to form a sauce.

5 Using a slotted spoon, transfer the pumpkin to a serving dish. Pour the sugary liquid from the pan over the pumpkin and serve at once with plain yogurt, sweetened with a little brown sugar, if desired.

Buñuelos

INGREDIENTS

Serves 6

2 cups all-purpose flour
1 teaspoon baking powder
½ teaspoon salt
1 tablespoon granulated sugar
1 large egg, beaten
½ cup milk
2 tablespoons unsalted butter,
   melted
oil, for frying
granulated sugar, for dusting

For the syrup

1⅓ cups light brown sugar
3 cups water
1-inch cinnamon stick
1 clove

1 Make the syrup. Combine all the ingredients in a saucepan. Heat, stirring, until the sugar has dissolved, then simmer until the mixture is reduced to a light syrup. Remove and discard the spices. Keep the syrup warm while you make the *buñuelos*.

2 Sift the flour, baking powder and salt into a bowl. Stir in the sugar. In a mixing bowl, whisk the egg and the milk well together. Gradually stir in the dry mixture, then beat in the melted butter to make a soft dough.

3 Turn the dough onto a lightly floured board and knead until it is smooth and elastic. Divide the dough into 18 even-size pieces. Shape into balls. With your hands, flatten the balls to disks about 2 inches thick.

4 Use the floured handle of a wooden spoon to poke a hole through the center of each *buñuelo*. Pour oil into a deep frying pan to a depth of 2 inches. Alternatively, use a deep-fryer. Heat the oil to 375°F, or until a cube of day-old bread added to the oil browns in 30–60 seconds.

─────── COOK'S TIP ───────

Make the syrup ahead of time if you prefer, and chill it until ready to use, when it can be warmed through quickly.

5 Fry the fritters in batches, taking care not to overcrowd the pan, until they are puffy and golden brown on both sides. Lift out with a slotted spoon and drain on paper towels.

6 Dust the *buñuelos* with sugar and serve with the syrup.

Almond Pudding with Custard

INGREDIENTS

Serves 6–8
1 cup water
1 envelope powdered gelatin
1 cup granulated sugar
½ teaspoon almond extract
6 egg whites
ground cinnamon, for dusting

For the custard
6 egg yolks
¼ cup granulated sugar
pinch of salt
2 cups light cream
½ teaspoon vanilla extract

1 Pour the water into a saucepan and sprinkle the gelatin over the surface. When it has softened, add the sugar and place the pan over low heat. Stir until both the gelatin and the sugar have completely dissolved.

2 Stir in the almond extract. Pour the mixture into a bowl, cool, then chill until it begins to thicken.

3 Whisk the egg whites in a dry, clean bowl until stiff peaks form.

4 Beat the gelatin mixture until it is frothy, then fold in the egg whites. Turn into a serving bowl and chill for several hours, or until firm.

5 Meanwhile, make the custard. Mix the egg yolks, sugar and salt in a double boiler or heavy saucepan. Add the cream and cook over very low heat, stirring constantly, until the custard coats the spoon.

6 Remove from the heat and stir in the vanilla extract. Cover the surface of the custard with dampened waxed paper to prevent a skin from forming. Cool, then chill. Serve with the pudding, dusted with cinnamon, if desired.

> ——— COOK'S TIP ———
>
> As soon as the custard coats the spoon, remove it from the heat; the custard will thin out if cooked beyond this point.

Coconut Custard

INGREDIENTS

Serves 6

1 cup sugar
1 cup water
3-inch cinnamon stick
1 cup grated fresh coconut
3 cups milk
4 eggs
³/₄ cup whipping cream
3 tablespoons toasted chopped
  almonds (optional)

1 Combine the sugar, water and cinnamon stick in a large saucepan. Bring to a boil, lower the heat and simmer, uncovered, for 5 minutes. Remove the cinnamon stick.

2 Add the grated coconut to the pan, and cook over low heat for 5 minutes more. Stir in the milk and cook, stirring from time to time, until the mixture has thickened to the consistency of thin custard. Remove from the heat and set aside.

3 Beat the eggs in a mixing bowl until fluffy. Add a small ladleful (about 3 tablespoons) of the coconut mixture to the eggs and stir to mix. Continue to add the coconut mixture in this way, then return the contents of the bowl to the clean pan. Stir well.

4 Cook over low heat, stirring constantly with a wooden spoon, until the mixture becomes a thick custard. Pour into a serving dish.

5 Cool the custard, then chill until ready to serve. Whip the cream until thick and spread it over the custard. Decorate with the toasted chopped almonds, if using.

COOK'S TIP

The easiest way to prepare a fresh coconut is to bake it in a preheated 350°F oven for 15 minutes, then pierce two of the eyes with an ice pick or sharp skewer. Drain the milk (and reserve). Open the coconut by hitting it carefully with a hammer; it will break into several pieces, making it easy to remove the shell. Peel off the inner brown skin, chop the flesh into small pieces and grate in a food processor.

DRINKS

Mexicans quench their thirst with a wide range of beverages, from the ancient corn drink atole *right through to the modern tequila cocktail, the Margarita.* Refrescos – *fruit drinks of various kinds – are very popular, as are beers, wines, liqueurs, rum and other tequila-based cocktails. Mexico is coffee and chocolate country and these beverages are prepared in a unique fashion. Some fruit drinks feature flowers, as when hibiscus sepals are used to make* Agua de Jamaica. Agua de Tamarindo *is made with tamarind pulp – and there are many other unusual and exotic drinks to discover in this fascinating country.*

Sangrita

INGREDIENTS

Serves 8
1 pound tomatoes, peeled, seeded
    and chopped
½ cup orange juice
4 tablespoons freshly squeezed
    lime juice
1 small onion, chopped
½ teaspoon granulated sugar
6 small fresh green chilies, seeded
    and chopped
Aged tequila (*Tequila Añejo*)
salt

— COOK'S TIP —

Plain white tequila is not suitable for this drink. Choose one of the amber aged tequilas (*añejos*), which are smoother and gentler on the palate.

1 Put the tomatoes, orange juice, lime juice, onion, sugar and green chilies in a food processor.

2 Process the tomato mixture until very smooth, scraping down the sides if necessary.

3 Pour the tomato mixture into a pitcher and chill well.

4 Pour into small glasses, allowing about 6 tablespoons per portion. Pour the tequila into small glasses, allowing 2 ounces per person. Sip the tomato juice and tequila alternately.

Sangria

This very popular summer drink was borrowed from Spain. The Mexican version is slightly lower in alcohol than the original.

INGREDIENTS

Serves 6
ice cubes
4 cups dry red table wine
⅔ cup freshly squeezed orange
    juice
¼ cup freshly squeezed lime
    juice
½ cup superfine sugar
2 limes or 1 apple, sliced, to serve

1 Half fill a large pitcher with ice cubes. Pour in the wine and the orange and lime juices.

2 Add the sugar and stir well until it has dissolved. Pour into tall glasses and float the lime slices on top. Serve at once.

— COOK'S TIP —

Sugar does not dissolve readily in alcohol. It is best to use simple syrup, which is very easy to make and gives a smoother drink. Combine 2 cups granulated sugar and 2 cups water in a pitcher and set aside until the sugar has dissolved. Stir from time to time. 1 tablespoon simple syrup is the equivalent of 1½ teaspoons sugar.

Rompope

This tasty drink could best be described as cooked eggnog. It keeps well if chilled but seldom lasts that long.

INGREDIENTS

Makes about 7½ cups
4 cups milk
1 cup granulated sugar
2-inch cinnamon stick
½ cup ground almonds
12 large egg yolks
2 cups golden rum

—————— COOK'S TIP ——————

Try serving this over lots of ice in a tall glass for a deliciously long drink.

---

1 Combine the milk, sugar and cinnamon in a large saucepan. Simmer over very low heat, stirring constantly, until the sugar has dissolved.

2 Cool to room temperature. Remove the cinnamon stick and stir in the ground almonds.

3 Beat the egg yolks in a bowl until they are very thick and pale.

4 Add the egg yolks to the almond mixture a little at a time, beating well. Return the pan to the heat and cook gently until the mixture coats a spoon. Cool.

5 Stir in the rum. Pour into a clean dry bottle and cork tightly. Keep in the fridge for 2 days before serving as an aperitif or liqueur.

Tequila Cocktail

The traditional way to drink tequila is to place some salt on the back of the left hand between the base of the thumb and index finger. Taking care not to spill the salt, hold a halved lime in the same hand. Then hold a small tequila glass in the right hand. Lick a little salt, down the tequila and immediately suck the juice from the lime.

INGREDIENTS
Serves 2
scant ½ cup white tequila
6 tablespoons freshly squeezed lime juice
2 tablespoons grenadine syrup
crushed ice
twists of lime rind, to serve

1 Combine the tequila, lime juice and grenadine syrup in a mixing glass and stir to mix thoroughly.

2 Fill two cocktail glasses three-quarters full with crushed ice and carefully pour the tequila cocktail into each glass. Serve each drink with one or two short drinking straws and a twist of lime rind.

Bloody Maria

INGREDIENTS

Serves 2

3/4 cup tomato juice
6 tablespoons white tequila
dash each Worcestershire and
    Tabasco sauces
2 tablespoons lemon juice
8 ice cubes
salt and freshly ground black pepper

— COOK'S TIP —

When drinks are to be served with ice,
make sure all the ingredients are thoroughly chilled ahead of time.

1 Combine the tomato juice, tequila, Worcestershire and Tabasco sauces, and lemon juice in a cocktail shaker. Add salt and pepper to taste, and four ice cubes. Shake very vigorously.

2 Place the remaining ice cubes in two heavy-based glasses and strain the tequila over them.

Margarita

Tequila is made from the sap of a fleshy-leafed plant called the blue agave and gets its name from the town of Tequila, where it has been made for more than 200 years. The Margarita is the most well-known drink made with tequila.

INGREDIENTS

Serves 2

1/2 lime or lemon
salt
1/2 cup white tequila
2 tablespoons Triple Sec or
    Cointreau
2 tablespoons freshly squeezed lime or
    lemon juice
4 or more ice cubes

— COOK'S TIP —

It really is worth going to the trouble of
buying limes for this recipe. Lemons will
do, but something of the special flavor of
the drink will be lost in the substitution.

1 Rub the rims of two cocktail glasses with the lime. Pour some salt into a saucer and dip in the glass rims so that they are frosted.

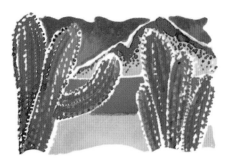

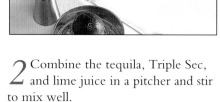

2 Combine the tequila, Triple Sec, and lime juice in a pitcher and stir to mix well.

3 Pour the tequila mixture into the prepared glasses. Add the ice cubes and serve at once.

Pot Coffee

In Mexico, *Cafe de Olla* is made with the local Mexican brown sugar, known as *piloncillo*. Dark brown sugar can be used and makes a fine substitute.

INGREDIENTS

Serves 4
4 cups water
²/₃ cup dark brown sugar
2-inch cinnamon stick
3 cloves
²/₃ cup medium-grind dark-roast coffee

1 Combine the water, brown sugar, cinnamon stick and cloves in a saucepan. Slowly bring to a boil over low heat. Stir occasionally until the sugar has dissolved completely.

2 Stir in the ground coffee and boil for 1 minute more. Remove from the heat, cover and let steep for about 5 minutes.

3 Strain the coffee through a fine sieve into small cups or mugs. Serve immediately.

Corn Drink with Milk

In Aztec times this drink – *Atole de Leche* – would have been made with plain water, since milk was not part of the diet until the Spanish introduced cattle into Mexico. It would have been sweetened with honey, or not sweetened at all, for sugar was another ingredient introduced by the Conquerors.

INGREDIENTS

Serves 6
½ cup *masa harina* (tortilla flour)
2 cups water
1 vanilla pod
4 cups milk
a little sugar

1 Combine the *masa harina* and the water in a large heavy saucepan, stirring to mix well. Add the vanilla pod and cook over low heat, stirring constantly, until the mixture has thickened.

2 Remove the pan from the heat and gradually stir in the milk. Sweeten with granulated sugar to taste.

3 Return the pan to the heat and cook for just long enough to heat through, stirring all the time. Remove the vanilla pod and serve the drink hot.

Chocolate Corn Drink

In Mexico, drinking chocolate is beaten with a very pretty carved wooden *molinillo,* but a wire whisk does the job just as well, if not so decoratively. This traditional drink also contains *masa harina* and is known in Mexico as *Champurrado.*

INGREDIENTS

Serves 6
½ cup *masa harina* (tortilla flour)
3 cups plain water
2-inch cinnamon stick
3 cups milk
3 squares Mexican chocolate, or any unsweetened (bitter) chocolate, grated
a little light brown sugar

1 Combine the *masa harina* and water in a large heavy saucepan, stirring to mix well. Add the cinnamon stick and cook, stirring, over low heat until the mixture has thickened.

—— COOK'S TIP ——

If Mexican chocolate isn't available, use unsweetened chocolate instead.

2 Gradually stir in the milk, then the grated chocolate. Continue to cook until all the chocolate has dissolved, beating with a whisk or a Mexican *molinollo.* Discard the cinnamon stick. Sweeten to taste with brown sugar. Serve hot in cups.

Mexican Hot Chocolate

INGREDIENTS

Serves 1
1 cup water or milk or a mixture of the two
1½ ounces Mexican chocolate or any bittersweet chocolate

1 Put the water or milk in a saucepan together with the chocolate and slowly bring to a simmer over low heat. Simmer, stirring continuously, until the chocolate has melted. Continue to heat gently for 4–5 minutes to blend the flavors.

2 Pour the chocolate into a bowl and beat with a *molinillo* (see above) until frothy. If a *molinillo* is not available, use a whisk or an electric mixer. Pour the chocolate into a mug and serve at once.

Rosella Drink

In Mexico, the bright red sepals of a tropical flowering plant, *Hibiscus sabdariffa*, are used to make drinks. Available fresh in the Caribbean at Christmas and dried at other times, the plant is known in Mexico as *Flor de Jamaica* and elsewhere as rosella or sorrel. This drink is known as *Agua de Jamaica*.

INGREDIENTS

Serves 4
4 cups water
2 ounces rosella sepals
a little sugar

— COOK'S TIP —

This soft drink can be made very festive with the addition of light rum. Mix 2 ounces light rum with an equal amount of Rosella Drink for each serving.

1 Combine the water and rosella sepals in a large saucepan. Bring to a boil over medium heat.

2 Boil gently, uncovered, for 1 minute, then remove from the heat and let stand for 15 minutes. Stir in a little sugar to sweeten to taste. Strain into a pitcher. Cool, then cover and chill very well.

3 Serve the ice-cold Rosella Drink in tall glasses filled with ice.

Tamarind Drink

INGREDIENTS

Serves 4
8 ounces tamarind pods
4 cups water
a little granulated sugar

— COOK'S TIP —

Tamarind pulp is sometimes sold in tropical markets and Indian or Asian stores. Sometimes it is available strained and concentrated, in which case you can bypass step 2, below.

1 Peel the tamarind pods and put them into a saucepan. Pour in the water and let soak for 4 hours.

2 Mash the tamarind pulp very well with a fork; remove and discard the seeds. Press the pulp through a sieve into a large bowl.

3 Sweeten the *Agua de Tamarindo* to taste. Pour into a pitcher and chill. Serve in tall glasses filled with ice.

Index